Re-imagining the Office

Re-imagining the Office

The New Workplace Challenge

ADRYAN BELL

GOWER

Published by
Gower Publishing Limited
Wey Court East
Union Road
Farnham
Surrey, GU9 7PT
England

Ashgate Publishing Company
Suite 420
101 Cherry Street
Burlington,
VT 05401-4405
USA

www.gowerpublishing.com

British Library Cataloguing in Publication Data
Bell, Adryan.
  Re-imagining the office : the new workplace challenge.
  1. Office layout. 2. Work environment.
  I. Title
  658.2'3-dc22

  ISBN: 978-0-566-08770-7

Library of Congress Cataloging-in-Publication Data
Bell, Adryan.
  Re-imagining the office : the new workplace challenge / by Adryan Bell.
      p. cm.
  Includes bibliographical references and index.
  ISBN 978-0-566-08770-7 (hbk.) 1. Office layout. 2. Work environment. 3. Organizational effectiveness. I. Title.
  HF5547.2.B45 2010
  651--dc22

                                                                    2009042660

Mixed Sources
Product group from well-managed forests and other controlled sources
www.fsc.org Cert no. SA-COC-1565
© 1996 Forest Stewardship Council
FSC

Printed and bound in Great Britain by
MPG Books Group, UK

Contents

About the Author

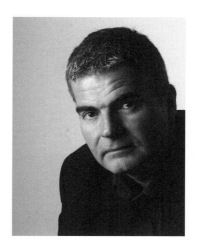

Adryan started his career as a civil servant, undertaking a variety of roles across locations and departments, as civil servants do. He also had a spell helping to run the family property renovation business for a few years. He joined the international workplace consultants DEGW in the mid-1990s, from the Government agency Scottish Enterprise, becoming Director of Workplace Strategy and Change. Whilst with DEGW, Adryan worked on a wide range of public and private sector projects, both within the UK and internationally – focusing particularly on the cultural change associated with the transitions to new work environments and new work practices. Adryan now works on a freelance basis, whilst pursuing other projects – including, most recently, taking up a senior part-time advisory role with the Northern Ireland Civil Service as Head of Work Innovation.

Adryan is married with four children (and a dog). He lives in Bristol, spending some of his time in Belfast. He has previously also lived and worked in London, Yorkshire and Scotland – enabling his children to develop some interesting accents! Adryan has authored or co-authored a number of books on workplace strategy and change and is a regular speaker at conferences on these themes. He has also had poetry and music published. His hobbies include travelling, playing guitar and piano, running an e-bay shop and driving quirky cars. His ambition is to write a novel.

Adryan Bell, future at work limited – adryan.bell@googlemail.com

Preface

Sitting on a covered terrace of a colonial-style hotel in Southern Thailand, looking out to sea and watching tropical rain and lightning at its best may seem an odd location to start to write a new book on the evolving office workplace. But sometimes, assisted by chance, you need to be somewhere very different to understand and see something very familiar, from a new and better perspective.

In committing to the idea of writing this book in the summer of 2008, I realised I needed to go somewhere a bit different with it – although travelling across the world was not exactly what I had in mind at the time!

My intention was to write a book that would be personal; as well as practical, accessible and relevant to its readers. I also wanted the book to excite and to stimulate new discussion for those involved in creating, managing or, simply, just working in offices, as so many of us do. I wanted to encourage a sense of challenge and exploration, and hopefully action. Certainly to question yesterday's workplace conventions, which are still so prevalent today; but also to challenge even today's so-called innovation. Are we really going far enough?

The stark contrast and isolation of the beautiful setting that I find myself in, arouses new thoughts about my relationship with work, location and the office desk. Armed, by today's standards, with relatively modest technology and an open mind, it seems in my own way I am leaving the world of the stereotypical office worker further and further behind. And I, of course, am not alone. And as the world of business around me continues to evolve and innovate in order to thrive and survive, it is becoming less clear what the future may hold for the office worker. But even more uncertain is what the future holds for the office workplace itself.

Far away from the humdrum of our everyday working lives, different priorities, innovative ideas, fresh insights and new resolutions can so often flow

along with the holiday wine and sunshine. But can something really tangible change as a result of such vacation-inspired questioning and reflection? I believe the time for really significant workplace change has come. I hope to explain the reasoning and ideas behind this statement through the chapters of this book.

It seemed I needed to escape the office for Thailand for my inspiration. Hopefully the book can help liberate your own thinking without the need to travel halfway round the world (and at a fraction of the cost) – although you will miss out on all that spectacular scenery and weather, I'm afraid…

Adryan Bell

Banner image, *source*: © Rushour | Dreamstime.com

Introduction

In considering the office workplace we cannot, and should not, detach it from the world around it. The world of business, as well as our everyday lives – both of which are being re-invented at their leading edges on a daily basis. Driven by relentless advances in technology, the fast changing economic landscape, as well as the more sedate, even subconscious, shifting of personal attitudes and values, we are all touched by change in our work and personal lives in some way or another these days, it seems.

Introduction

Changing times

In considering the office workplace we cannot, and should not, detach it from the world around it. The world of business, as well as our everyday lives – both of which are being re-invented at their leading edges on a daily basis. Driven by relentless advances in technology, an ever changing economic landscape, as well as the more sedate, even subconscious, shifting of personal attitudes and values, we are all touched by change in our work and personal lives in some way or another these days, it seems.

If, like me, you have had the pleasure of working in an office environment during the past 15–20 years or so – think back to your earliest, pre-personal computer, pre-e-mail experiences. It's almost impossible to make comparisons with a typical *'day in the office'* now. The pace and scale of an individual's office-work today is dramatically different – but, hold on, because things are not about to settle down. Demand and expectation will likely increase further. Our most critical work skills in the future may be our ability and discipline to assert order and control to our working lives, so we don't burn out and can get that elusive work/life balance right.

We have all probably at some time ridiculed aspects of our parent's outlook on life. Their generation, of course, grew up with very different influences, values and priorities. The scary thing is that our children will, or more likely already do, view us with that same air of bemusement.

Absorbed as I am now in my world of 'anywhere e-mail and internet', courtesy of my i-phone or my wireless laptop, I was recently taking my father, who is now in his eighties, through his first steps in using e-mail and the Internet, allowing him to belatedly join the technology revolution. We were both abruptly brought back down to earth, however, by my '24/7 text-messaging' teenage son who informed us, quite seriously, that 'e-mail is for old people'. It hurt a bit – but the thing is, I know he's probably right. It's not just

my father who is struggling too keep up with today's technology.

But, of course, there is much more to the future of work than technology, which we need to exploit, but not be driven by. The energy and ideas of youth need to be balanced with the knowledge and wisdom of business

> **'Our most critical work skills in the future may be our ability and discipline to assert order and control to our working lives...'**

and life experience. There are probably four generations now shaping the workplace, all with a potential role to play. It won't be easy to get it right.

We are certainly living in changing times. And, it seems, change is not new; we often absorb it without even noticing. But it is the pace and scope of change today that is arguably unprecedented.

So how do we make sense of the changes in commerce, technology, lifestyles and demographics that lie ahead for us? Do we need to embrace all these changes or can we get away by watching from the sidelines, if we want to? Whilst recognising that change and improvement is not necessarily the same thing; opting out of change is not as easy as we would like either. In a business sense, failure to embrace change and innovation has proven to be fatal. Where does the office workplace fit into this world of change and survival?

It is clear that the office workplace cannot exist in isolation from this wider context; although in many senses, it has done just that for decades. So, too, have those that have built careers, services and products around it. If we are to collectively create the right sort of workplaces for the right sorts of organisations in the future, real appreciation of the way business, technology and social dynamics are changing and inter-relating will, I believe, be essential. And this understanding will be as important as any knowledge about architecture or design. However, it would seem that we are often blind to this bigger picture, as we each follow the rituals of our daily work routines.

It seems that the physical workplace has become, for many, a comfortable time warp; encouraging a risk-adverse, out-dated way of doing business. Sure, we have made advances here and there, but will such tinkering around at the edges in the future be enough? Perhaps we really do now need to come out of this 'comfort zone'. Create some (albeit perhaps temporary) discomfort. We need to be more creative and imaginative. We need to forget the past and embrace a very different, if uncertain future.

Challenging workplace conventions

More specifically, I believe we need to challenge and re-invent many existing long-standing workplace conventions. These include basic aspects like office design and image, workplace status and symbolism, dependency on desks, use of alternative worksettings and locations, 'territorialism', use of paper, exploitation of technology and flexibility with time. More fundamentally, we need to actually challenge the whole concept and location of the workplace – and its role in supporting our work and the organisations we work for.

I believe that, well within the next decade, we will reached a pivotal point in the evolution of business and the nature of work, enabled by technology and the Internet, as well as, importantly, our new values and expectations. We will move from years of theory and speculation about the future to a new, perhaps unrecognisable, reality. Enlightened, networked individuals will realise and embrace this change first; taking with them smaller, agile organisations. More established larger organisations will then need to embrace the changes or face decline as the speed of change becomes merciless.

The workplace that survives will need to be a very different place too, and fulfil a very different role.

Changing minds, as well as offices

The biggest challenges in this context, as always, will be ones around mindsets and attitudes. Overcome the limitations here – and the rest will follow. We, increasingly, will have new responsibilities as individuals to find our place in this new world, as no one else will do it for us. Changing deep-rooted mindsets and behaviours, however, will not be easy. It never has been.

I once worked hard to climb corporate ladders to secure the workplace trappings of personal rank and status that I thought were important. At some point, I left it all behind. The penny dropped. I now see and use the workplace, my work and my working relationships in a very different way. I can hardly remember how this happened – but I know it wasn't forced. I found it out for myself. And that self-discovery is the key to the process we need to initiate if we are to achieve the wholesale attitude change required as part of this challenge.

The physical workplace itself, of course, can have an active role to play in this transformation. As have those responsible for its creation. The new workplace (in whatever form that takes) need not be simply an outcome of change, but, like technology, a pro-active enabler of it. Aside from its functional role, physical form has always had a strong influence on mood and behaviours, as well as being a symbol of evolving trends and new thinking.

I believe the concept of physical 'place' will be more important than ever, despite our increasingly virtual existences. But it must be the right 'place', conveying the right messages and providing the right experiences for its users. People will continue to be the key ingredient in any future workplace – and their use and acceptance of it will dictate its success or failure.

> **'Changing deep-rooted mindsets and behaviours, however, will not be easy. It never has been.'**

But what do we need to change? What conventional, or indeed newly emerging,

workplace concepts will still continue to apply? What do we need to do to prepare for, and respond to, this challenge?

Re-imagining the office

In many respects, we can only really imagine what sort of office workplace, where required, will need to exist in the longer term to support this new world and the future nature of work and business. But imagine, or to be more accurate – re-imagine, we must. And we must start now. Even if we only get it part-right or part-implemented – we will still be one crucial step ahead of all those who fail to see the need for radical change.

Many people have been sceptical about the sort of workplaces I believe we need to start creating. Many see current innovations only as a move to a one-size-fits-all, cloned, cost-driven working environment. Such developments are, however, open to different interpretations.

I advocate the very opposite. Very special, unique places that need proper investment to ensure they are attractive, stimulating and highly effective. Places that allow us to be as individual as we like, in terms of our chosen workstyles. Places where people want to be and where the experience of being there is rewarding, though perhaps not through satisfaction in the sense many of us might apply today. Places that harness relevant technologies but are not hampered by its complexity or fallacies. Places that provide that illusive added-value that will make the difference and set organisations apart.

Part of the challenge will be to instil a sense of trust, understanding and belief in the workplace of the future and the associated process of change. We need to be skilled change agents if we are to bring people positively along with us. This may only be a transitional challenge, however, as much of today's emerging workforce, like my children, will anticipate, or rather demand, these changes as part of a more fluid career and work-life balance expectation.

If we don't provide and be part of the right solution, they will create it for themselves. Far from change agents, we ourselves will be the potential barriers to innovation.

Starting from scratch

A blank sheet of paper may be the best place to start the design process for the new workplace. This way, we will not be distracted by what has gone before. It is for this reason that, increasingly, architects without relevant sector experience are being selected to bring about a fresh perspective to projects. If all a particular architect has ever designed is hospitals or schools, for example, are they best placed to provide desired or required innovation? Likewise, vast experience in office design may not be as valuable as first suggested. Design of hotels, shopping malls or even master-planning of cities may be more relevant.

In a similar way, the future office workplace itself can be seen as a 'blank canvas' for its users – the new 'level playing field' on which we, as users, must learn to be different as individuals, teams and networks; through our ideas, actions and attitudes. Personalisation and individuality will be far from dead; it will just manifest itself in different ways and be even more relevant.

> **'A blank sheet of paper may be the best place to start the design process for the new workplace.'**

Such a workplace can become a liberated environment where what you do, not who you are, is what is important. Where you choose how and where you do your work. A place where dozens, or even hundreds, of different chosen workstyles can co-exist in harmony – from different teams, perhaps often even different organisations. A far, far cry from the feared cloned workplace, you will agree.

And if this all sounds a millions miles away from the office and working environments most of us recognise today – it probably is. But this is the scale of the new workplace challenge we now face.

The e-office

I aim to explore all these ideas in this book through six inter-related themes, all conveniently starting with 'e'. Each 'e' sequentially takes us further through conventional considerations around the office into the future. I make no apologies in taking a look back, as well as forward in doing this – it helps to provide the necessary context and reminders. We can learn from the past. And we should not throw everything completely away in boldly pursuing, as we must do, the new future.

The six 'e' themes are as follows:

- **Efficiency** – the original driver of workplace change, which still has a vital role to play in its future.

- **Effectiveness** – the balance to efficiency that can help ensure the workplace remains both functional and relevant in an uncertain future.

- **Engagement** – the process of appropriately involving staff in the workplace change process through clear leadership and sensitive change management – key to making workplace developments work and last.

- **Expression** – the messages the workplace conveys though its physical design and symbolism, to attract, inform, stimulate and motivate its users.

- **E-work** – a new word (possibly!) – to describe the future, ever-more virtual (place and organisation-independent) work practices, work patterns and

career models that will come to exist, enabled by technology, which the future office workplace will need to align with; and

- **Experience** – the sum of all the parts – the emotions that will define and differentiate the office workplace as a destination of choice and value, amidst the competing options that will be available to tomorrow's workers.

Collectively I suppose this adds up to the e-office, whatever that might mean. 'Electronic' was the original meaning of the 'e-' prefix in this context, introducing new terms such as e-mail, e-commerce and e-bay into our language. The e-prefix has come to imply much more than that, however, as our use and application of technology and electronic data becomes more and more sophisticated.

To look at this from a different angle, however, I like the 'e' term 'extraordinary' – because an office workplace, like so many other products and services in the future, will fail if it only manages to be ordinary. The expression 'business as unusual'[1] comes to mind here. Being distinguishable and being able to cater for niche needs will be essential in the future. Think about the impact of the Internet on our shopping habits and options (especially the likes of Amazon and eBay). This means being different, agile, adept and adaptable – and yes, even extraordinary. How does your current office environment measure up to this aspiration?

Making the difference

I also like the e-term 'emotive' – linking to my sixth 'e' experience theme. It is probably not the most obvious word we would associate with an office today, unless applied in the negative sense. But all that has to change. We will

---

1   Quotation from the publication 'Funky Business' – Kjell A. Nordström and Jonas Ridderstråle 1999; also title of publication by Anita Roddick, 2007.

increasingly make choices around our lives and work based on our hearts, as well as our minds – because that will be the differentiating factor.

Think about our choice (and the extent of our choice) around restaurants, holidays, homes or cars today. What really drives our decisions here? Work will be no different. Such need for differentiation emphasises the importance of new design, as well as new organisational, thinking – as those providing our chosen restaurants, holidays, hotels and cars have already learnt. The expression 'winning over hearts and minds' has never been more relevant in the workplace context. Like art, good design and expression has the power to unlock our emotions – adding unique and powerful value to physical form.

Disturbing the present

I believe attention to all of the 'e' themes outlined is now required, as part of a wider, essential business and cultural transformation for all organisations. The emphasis needs to be less on changing what we know, but more on creating what we don't know. And the workplace, as a physical entity, has the potential to play a key part in creating this new world for work.

> 'We will increasingly make choices around our lives and work based on our hearts, as well as our minds – because that will be the differentiating factor.'

The risks of getting it not quite right are high, but then even more so are the risks of non-action. It won't be easy. It won't be comfortable. Looking at the future disturbs the present.[2] But we can no longer afford to stand still and be consumed into the past.

---

2   Quote from Gaston Berger – French futurist.

I cannot claim to be able to provide all the answers or solutions in this book – we need to imagine and work through these ourselves; but perhaps, in the workplace context at least, I can provide some of the clues.

And rather than doom and gloom, I see nothing but opportunity here – at least for those of us who can be enlightened and can play an active part in the process. Whatever your role or interest, I hope that will be you. Good luck!

Efficiency

I can remember, back in the 1980s, when efficiency was King. Along with its cousins of total quality management and continuous business improvement (and all their associated badges!), it was like a newly discovered secret to business and organisational success. And it definitely had its moment and made its impact. In the context of the office workplace, there was much to be gained – and many careers and reputations prospered, at least in the short term, on the back of the belated 'discovery' of workplace efficiency.

1 Efficiency

Efficiency is king

I can remember, back in the 1980s, when efficiency was King. Along with its cousins of total quality management and continuous business improvement (and all their associated badges!), it was like a newly discovered secret to business and organisational success. And it definitely had its moment and made its impact. In the context of the office workplace, there was much to be gained – and many careers and reputations prospered, at least in the short term, on the back of the belated 'discovery' of workplace efficiency.

Years of tradition and self-protection had resulted in the office environment barely changing through its hundred-year or so history. Remarkable it would seem, particularly given the social and economic changes of the 1950s, 60s and 70s. If anything, things got worse, at least in terms of the quality and style of office buildings being provided (in my opinion, office and residential architecture of the 60s and 70s represented an all-time low in the industry). But the advent of wholesale computerisation from the 1980s was setting new challenges and the first real workplace revolution was overdue.

However, in many respects, this revolution failed to materialise – with efficiency drives, almost as a sideline, being the only real outcome. With some exceptions, business and work processes, working practices, workplace layouts, workplace culture and so on, all remained amazingly intact. It was as if, literally, computers were placed on desks to replace typewriters or paper, and that was it (although arguably the latter was never replaced); and this inaction has, without doubt, contributed to the bigger challenge we face today.

But at least there was the efficiency drives. And in the workplace context this took on a number of guises. Workspace (or

> '...the advent of wholesale computerisation from the 1980s was setting new challenges and the first real workplace revolution was overdue.'

accommodation as it is often referred to) was, and perhaps unfortunately still is, considered primarily a business overhead. And like all overheads, in the interest of efficiency, there is always a strong demand to cut back, wherever possible. If the amount of workspace could be reduced or the need to take on more workspace to accommodate growth be eliminated, then there were substantial costs to be saved, especially in more expensive city centre locations.

Years of scant regard to organisational costs unveiled sudden new potential here. Perhaps not surprisingly, the focus was on quick and easy wins primarily, with many, perhaps more serious, aspects of workplace efficiency still overlooked. Moreover, the focus on the workplace meant too often that some of the wider, more challenging business and organisational efficiency challenges were not faced or even recognised.

The hatchet was out

Nevertheless, the workplace hatchet was out. Space allocations (standards) per person were cut, but often typically not for senior management. So-thought 'luxury' spaces like training rooms or breakout spaces were re-configured as workspace. Meetings rooms too were reduced and the space retrenched.

Those ruthless enough went further. Where accommodation was predominately cellular, walls were removed and greater open-plan created; although again often not for those at the most senior management level in the organisation. These changes were crude in their implementation, with little thought of the implication for occupants or their work processes or re-thinking of the design of the resultant workplace.

More extreme actions followed though into the early 90s, notably in the telecoms, technology and management consultancy sectors. Hundreds of staff, typically sales staff or consultants, were given laptops (the size of concrete blocks in those days!) in place of desks and were sent on the road to pioneer

early remote working. Whole floors were emptied. Whole buildings decanted.

Offices were merged and accommodation rationalised. Estate strategies were re-written. Big cost reductions and savings were achieved. Conferences, books and new consultancies emerged from nowhere to exploit this new 'incredible' discovery. But in-credible, in many ways, it was.

> **'These changes were crude in their implementation, with little thought of the implication for occupants or their work processes...'**

Efficiency mistakes and misuse

It was a one-off – as there was always going to be limit to such basic asset-stripping, particularly with its short-term, immediate focus – and in many cases it went too far, with staff morale and productivity taking a dive.

To their credit, the telecoms, computer and management consultancy organisations quickly recognised their mistakes and re-instated new forms of office facilities for their remote workers. They were the first to pioneer, albeit crudely, formalised hot-desking arrangements; where less desks than people were provided, with desks being shared, typically on a bookable basis. This important innovation provided an insight into an aspect of workplace efficiency which only now is starting to be properly understood, refined and exploited effectively.

I shall return to the topic of desk-sharing frequently in this book. The desk is, in many ways, the ultimate symbol of the conventional office workplace, representing perhaps the last taboo for workplace change. Anyone who has tried moving, let alone *re*-moving an individual's desk will testify this. It is a brave person who can confidently declare 'the desk is dead'; but perhaps inevitably it will be, at least in the sense that most see a dedicated desk today.

Efficiency in context

But of course workplace efficiency on its own is relatively insignificant. Workplace costs typically represent only a minor portion, around 10 per cent, of the total cost of running an organisation, with the 'people cost' accounting for around six times this amount.

'...“the desk is dead”...'

From this, you can quickly see how only a very small percentage improvement in employee efficiency or productivity can yield much more significant benefits.

The bigger prize, without doubt, is in these broader organisational and operational efficiencies and improvements – and in then taking the next step to appropriately re-design the workplace to reflect and support those changes. Such re-design will then naturally bring about its own efficiencies, but as an outcome not a driver of change. Indeed to approach workplace re-design in any other way is, arguably, like allowing the 'tail to wag the dog'.

It does appear that across so many organisations, even today, over-bureaucratic, hierarchal and complex business and organisational structures and processes are still yet to be significantly tackled. Even where these elements have been 're-engineered' (another potentially superficial, business trend), there was little connection to the working environment as an enabler to what was trying to be achieved. In most cases, though barely recognised, the workplace became a hindrance to change. Important opportunities were lost.

These early efficiency drives also gave workplace modernisation and open-plan working and hot-desking, in particular, a bad name; creating a negative reputation that was to stick in corporate memories for some time. Even today, these prejudices, based on genuine bad experiences for many, still exist – and are a curse to those trying to introduce workplace innovation.

I am not alone now in deliberately avoiding the use of words like 'open-plan' or 'hot-desking' when advising and supporting organisations through

workplace change, because of the connotations associated with these concepts. This, of course, has given rise to a whole lexicon of new buzzwords and trendy alternative terms for these concepts and other workplace initiatives. Although providing potentially more ammunition for the sceptics, such new language does allow an element of positive personalisation, even fun, to be applied to workplace initiatives.

> **'...the workplace became a hindrance to change.'**

Problem or cause?

I recently worked with a Government Agency who, because of unexpected operational changes and a resultant need for growth in staff numbers, found that it's new, yet to be completed, headquarters was going to be too small. Rather than compromise the important objectives of the new workplace, which was about bringing the organisation together under one roof for the first time, it bravely introduced desk-sharing arrangements as a means of accommodating the growth.

This approach was based on research which identified a modest level of empty desks on most days because of leave, sickness, training and so on; as well as the belief that the new, more dynamic, work environment being introduced would see a further increase of non-desk time. The organisation also allowed teams to create their own 'model' for sharing – some where everybody participated, others where specific people only were affected. Nevertheless, culturally this was not an easy task at all.

In many respects, I applaud the principles and innovation here and believe that scope for desk-sharing was a valid area to explore. However, the circumstances facing the organisation at that time did not, in my mind, represent the strongest rationale for introducing this sensitive concept. It was certainly a high-risk strategy.

Nevertheless, such a workspace solution, despite its challenges, may have been the easy way out. Was the real challenge to be faced one of staff numbers and associated business focus? As new areas of work open up, did others close down? Was re-training, as well as recruitment, considered properly? Was the problem, almost unfairly, presented to the property or accommodation team to solve? Did the organisation address the problem, but not the cause? It would be unfair to draw out any conclusions here but the situation certainly provides some food for thought.

The importance of hard efficiency

The positive aspect of the 1980s/90s efficiency movement was that real tangible cost reductions were attainable. As a result, office accommodation caught the eye of the Board, in a positive sense, perhaps for the first time. And the ability to make the case for related investment, for example in new furniture or more appropriate technology, became possible.

Over time, however, it has become very clear that the real benefits of workplace innovation lies not in the cost savings – which ideally become outcomes, rather than objectives of a workplace initiative – but in the broader, largely less tangible benefits of enabling more effective working and business operation. I shall explore this further in the next *effectiveness* chapter.

However, the short-term cost benefits, enabled through efficiency savings, still play an important role in securing business case approvals to embark on most workplace change projects. Unless you are lucky enough to have a very confident and enlightened leader or Board, the security of a project that can 'wash its face' in relatively immediate tangible financial terms, will always be an attractive proposition. Skilful exploitation of the hard efficiency potential of

> **'...office accommodation caught the eye of the Board...'**

workplace change is therefore still important in enabling workplace innovation to progress, which in turn allows the softer, less tangible but more significant effectiveness benefits to be realised over time.

Taking efficiency to the next level

Whilst I may have painted a picture of perhaps savage exploitation of workplace efficiency, it is worth recognising that this is not necessarily a universal situation. I am aware from many of my current consultancy assignments that a number of organisations are still discovering the basic and perhaps now, obvious, workplace efficiencies – first exploited 20 or so years back. This is particularly the case of smaller organisations and in many parts of the public sector, including local Government.

These organisations have the advantage of learning the lessons from the pioneers and thus have the potential for making significant progress. Furthermore, there are more sophisticated aspects to workplace efficiency that they can also consider – much of it previously overlooked or unavailable. Let me explain what I mean.

Desks and layouts

Shaving space standards and knocking down walls can provide some easy quick wins. Taking a hard look at the office layouts or space planning can also be fruitful. Very often the layouts of offices have evolved over time in a very organic and piece-meal way and have become somewhat illogical.

One key area is circulation. Although an important requirement, often there is inefficient or unnecessary space allowed for the movement of people around the workplace. Duplication of main circulation routes is common, particularly where offices have been removed. A professional re-plan of the office layout can yield important space savings here – allowing space to be freed up for

more workspace or, perhaps more importantly, some alternative support spaces (which perhaps have been previously removed in an over-zealous quest for efficiency).

> **'...working space quickly got filled, in many cases, with paper, files, manuals, storage trays, teddies, toys and general clutter...'**

Desk-sharing can also provide huge workspace efficiencies, but as alluded to earlier, needs to be implemented with care. I believe the driver for desk-sharing should primarily be about providing the most relevant and effective working environment, rather than be purely efficiency driven. For this reason I shall cover this topic in more detail in the next chapter.

'Giving something back' is a welcomed outcome of any workplace efficiency drive. Too often such initiatives have been used purely to save money and are very clearly seen as that from a staff point of view. Whilst there is nothing wrong with this, care needs to be taken around how far you can go with this without giving something back in return – for example, an improvement in quality or choice of new alternative worksettings within the more efficient workplace.

Another interesting area is that of desk-style. Traditionally desks have come in all sorts of shapes and sizes and can be put together in clusters in different ways – some desks and cluster arrangements being more space efficient than others. The characteristics of the desk have been driven partly by the need to accommodate technology – for example, the corner or 'L'-shaped desk which allowed a computer processor, plus a (until recently, quite chunky) computer screen and a keyboard and mouse. At the time of the early introduction of computers, the need for extensive paperwork and writing was still envisaged, thus warranting the need for extensive working space also. The fact that such working space quickly got filled, in many cases, with

paper, files, manuals, storage trays, teddies, toys and general clutter, is another matter, of course.

Desks characteristics were also driven by status, be it simply size and quality or add-ons, like 'wings' that act as a meeting tables, reflecting the importance of the occupant and the nature of their work. Many senior people also had, or still have, separate meeting tables to complement their desks, as well as more informal seating. Where they have their own room, this serves to justify that extravagance. Where this occurs in open-plan, it eats up valuable space and restricts space planning options – creating highly visible, but often unhelpful, symbols of status.

With the increasing use of flat screen technology and off-desk computer processors – either in a sling beneath the desk or even away from the desk completely where 'thin client'[1] arrangements are in place (where a small unit the size of a CD player is all that is required at the workstation) – the sizes of desks can now become smaller and straighter (bench style), albeit sometimes with some curvature for aesthetic reasons. This new style of desk offers infinitely more efficiency and flexibility in terms of layout and adaptation.

An Edinburgh-based bank recently realised a 40 per cent floor space saving across three floors of its headquarter's building, simply by changing to a more modern desking solution. That saving enabled new support worksettings to be introduced, as well as accommodate a modest increase in occupancy, and took away completely the notion that an alternative, bigger building was required (and all the disruption and added cost that implied). The change has also been the catalyst for a re-examination of desk allocation and an exploration of desk-sharing options.

Interestingly, the limit to space rationalisation and increased occupancy here was finally determined by considerations like fire regulations and toilet

---

1   Thin client – small-form desktop technology that requires no PC processor at the desk and links to centralised server-based processing (similarities with 1970s mainframe/dumb terminal arrangements).

provision, rather than ultimately what might be achieved through new furniture or new work practices. In this sense, the nature and characteristics of the building and its floor plates (and their planning efficiency), will always be a major consideration in driving overall workplace efficiency.

The generic workplace

Another efficiency approach worthy of mention is the creation of 'generic workspace', rather than workspace that is heavily adapted or personalised for a particular department, team or, indeed, set of individuals. The benefit here is in reduced 'churn' or change costs should the occupants change. Ideally, for example, if one team moves out of a workspace, another team can move in without the need to shift or change the furniture, technology, storage and so on. In these circumstances, the cost and ease of such 'churn' is minimal, as is business disruption. In contrast, traditionally such churn can often involve moving vast amounts of furniture and equipment, as well as the removal and/ or erection of partitions and other fixtures. This is often done simply to meet the whims of senior personnel eager to retain status or match inappropriate expectations, rather than support true business requirements.

The reality is that the requirements of different teams are probably broadly very similar, with a small range of common workstyles needing to be accommodated. The need to support different workstyles, as opposed to specific teams, is however very valid. This certainly isn't about 'one size fits all'. Within a generic workspace there should be a range of worksettings and associated functionality, enabling large numbers of workers with varying workstyles to operate successfully and harmoniously. I shall say more about aligning workspace with workstyles in the next chapter.

> '...the creation of "generic workspace"...'

Storage and printers

Two other areas of efficiency not addressed in the initial drives of the 80s and 90s, were that of storage provision and printers. In fairness, only more recently have there been viable scope for improvements here – in terms of reliable electronic document management systems, effective scanning and robust multi-device printer/scanner/copier equipment. As always, the technical and physical solutions are only part of the picture, and the cultural adjustments around providing reduced storage and sharing printers cannot be understated.

Nowadays, it is fairly typical to find new workplace projects implementing new storage standards of around one linear metre of personal storage and the equivalent of two linear metres of team/project storage, per person. For many organisations this can present a huge challenge and needs to be considered as a major change project in itself, perhaps linked to the introduction of new document management or archiving systems. But it also presents a fantastic opportunity to clear out unnecessary filing and clutter and improve the look and feel, as well as flexibility, of the workspace.

The move to shared printers is always an emotive one, particularly where staff have been used to having either their own printer or at least sharing with only a small number of people (and, significantly, having it very close by). Confidentiality is often cited as part of the pushback also. However, the improvements in functionality (including management of confidential printing), quality and speed – to say nothing of the environmental benefits of reduced equipment – quickly speak for themselves and this is an area where I have never experienced long-term resistance. The gained space that all those printers took up is a further benefit in terms of workspace efficiency and aesthetics.

Make your mark

I mentioned earlier the 'tail wagging the dog'. Interestingly, some of the most important business and cultural organisational transformations I have come

across have been led and enabled through workplace projects. Though not always intended from the outset, I have seen many organisations, or rather enlightened individuals or leadership, quickly recognise the catalyst influence that a workplace change project can present and seize the considerable wider organisational opportunities that are available.

Some of the most recent significant blue-chip company re-location or co-location projects have been used in this way, as have many of the recent Central Government re-location and workplace refurbishment projects, often funded under the Private Finance Initiative (PFI) arrangements.

These workplace projects have found ways of linking their own objectives and outcomes to wider organisational objectives and vision – often helping to join up disparate organisational initiatives, such as business strategy, technology or HR-based programmes. Although starting off typically from a workplace efficiency basis, the potential for wider benefits has been identified and senior sponsorship of these aims secured. These projects have also, I believe, helped present a more logical, tangible and holistic view of organisational change to the workforce. In these days of initiative and change overload this is both refreshing and helpful.

> **'Real heroes... have emerged...'**

Real heroes, in my mind, have emerged from the often undervalued property and facilities management disciplines to initiate powerful organisational change projects in this context. Often working alongside, but occasionally working in spite of, more obvious internal organisational change partners.

The lesson for organisational change agents here? You are possibly unaware that your most powerful change tool is around you – your office environment. Something that will either greatly support or significantly hinder what you are trying to achieve. Seize the opportunity to see more than just efficiency benefits from workplace change. Become a workplace hero or heroine yourself!

Effectiveness

As we have learnt, workplace efficiency, powerful as it can be, also has its limits. But balance it with the objective of creating both a more efficient *and effective* workplace, and then the potential and benefits for the organisation and its workforce can be really substantial.

Indeed, focusing on effectiveness as the prime driver will bring appropriate levels of efficiency with it by default. But what do we mean by workplace effectiveness?

2 Effectiveness

The effective organisation

As we have learnt, workplace efficiency, powerful as it can be, also has its limits. But balance it with the objective of creating both a more efficient *and effective* workplace, and then the potential and benefits for the organisation and its workforce can be really substantial.

Indeed, focusing on effectiveness as the prime driver will bring appropriate levels of efficiency with it by default. But what do we mean by workplace effectiveness?

In reality, we are talking about organisational effectiveness – where an organisation can deliver its business objectives successfully, supported by the optimal tools and resources. This includes a skilled and motivated workforce, the most appropriate technologies, appropriate and adaptable working practices and a relevant, fit-for-purpose, responsive working environment. The office workplace, in whatever form it eventually takes, is therefore a significant factor here. Not least because of its influential effect on so many other drivers of effectiveness, including the mood and attitude of the workforce itself.

Above all, a workplace has to support the work being undertaken by an organisation and its workforce, in whatever form, shape or distribution that organisation might take. The nature of work has changed significantly in recent decades and, as we shall explore in the chapters ahead, will continue to change, perhaps unrecognisably. But let's just reflect on where we have come from and where we are now in this respect, before looking further into the future.

Desk-based mindset

The office workplace has, almost since its inception, placed its emphasis on the desk. Be it within an open-plan-style environment, within a large enclosed space or (for some) within a dedicated (single-occupancy) room. From the desk,

staff were expected to perform the majority of their duties, apart from when in meetings (which in some cases could be a substantial part of their time). To support this 'additional requirement' separate enclosed meeting rooms, of varying sizes, were typically provided, or meeting tables provided within the larger dedicated offices. I appreciate there were exceptions here – for specialist or customer-facing roles, for example – but

> **'...the desk is actually a compromise, suitable only for some tasks, some of the time.'**

for the majority of the workforce, the desk, supported by meeting rooms, was essentially the basis of the office workplace for decades.

As the nature of work has evolved and diversified over time, the ability to effectively perform the majority of tasks at the desk, particularly in a shared, open environment, has become questionable. This is especially true when staff are not all in the same activity-mode as each other at the same time: for example, when some are collaborating or taking phone calls whilst others are trying to read or concentrate. As well as compromises around noise, distraction and interruption, the desk also has its limitations in terms of ability to support certain tasks – for example, working with others, working with large amount of papers or reference materials or working with specialist equipment. As soon as the nature of our work moves away from the more routine, individual process work, which technology has largely taken away for many of us, the desk is actually a compromise, suitable only for some tasks, some of the time.

A room of your own

Of course, this is why those who are used to having their own dedicated office can be so reluctant to let them go. And you can understand why. Those with large enough dedicated offices often had, as well as a desk, their own meeting table, even soft seating – providing the best of all worlds, in terms of a range of worksetting choices to match different modes of work and degrees of

collaboration. However, as we are also aware, such a set-up is highly inefficient, if dedicated to one person.

For one thing, typically, such senior staff are rarely in the office and, even when they are, they can only usefully use one component of that room at any one time. Also, often the very nature of such dedicated rooms can create division and isolation, inhibiting the benefits of serendipitous encounters and interaction, so important in today's workplace. It is also not very inclusive, with only the lucky few (usually the most senior staff) enjoying such facilities, which in truth the majority of the workforce would equally find useful.

The other downside of the dedicated office is the way that, in many buildings, they are typically positioned around outside walls to maximise the views. Great for those based in those rooms, less impressive for those left in the gloomier interior (often open-plan) workspace, denied of daylight, views and perhaps even fresh air; exasperating an often unhelpful status divide. Especially unfair as these people would tend to be based in the office more than the dedicated office-dwellers. Alternatively, in narrower buildings, such outside offices tend to create long, barren central corridors. With their lines of closed doors, these can be lonely places even in the middle of a busy day; a far cry from the desired interactive, dynamic workplace.

In more recent times, the positioning of enclosed spaces/rooms near to core areas (like lifts, stairs and toilets) or in the deeper internal space, has helped provide better quality of open workspace. More extensive use of glass partitioning also supports a greater sense of light, openness and integration. Culturally, many senior staff have also become sensitive to the status imbalance and have 'opened up' their offices for others to use when they are not in or given them up altogether. Other gestures like keeping doors open (or even removing them entirely) support the move to a more egalitarian workplace.

> **'Open-plan became a bad word.'**

This is all part of a broader trend towards a more open working environment for all staff, at all levels, which undoubtedly can provide many effectiveness benefits for the organisation in terms of enhanced communication, collaboration and team working. Indeed these are aspects of work which would likely have been severely stifled by the more traditional, hierarchical working environment.

As with so many workplace trends, however, the early drives towards open work environments were at times crude – taking down walls without any re-thought of how the resultant space would work in practice. Huge prairie-style office environments were created as a result, making it impossible for many to work effectively in. Open-plan became a bad word.

The landscaped office

I have always urged caution around the complete removal of all enclosed spaces in the quest of creating the desired modern, open working environments. We all recognise that whilst open-plan has its benefits, it can also make certain tasks, particularly those that require quiet and concentration, less effective. Places to retreat and hide are as important as places to interact and be seen. On many occasions I have heard people tell me that they either work from home or work very early or late in the office, not because they want to, but because this is the only way they can get certain aspects of their work done. In my mind, the office workplace has failed these people, big time.

Interestingly, when my former employers DEGW[1] modernised its previous Crinan Street, London head office in the mid-1990s, it deliberately created more enclosed space. It also greatly increased the amount of shared workspace, over owned space, provided, and interestingly created a new category of 'temporary owned space' to support project-based team-working. See Figure 2.1.

---

1   DEGW, international workplace consultants – www.degw.com.

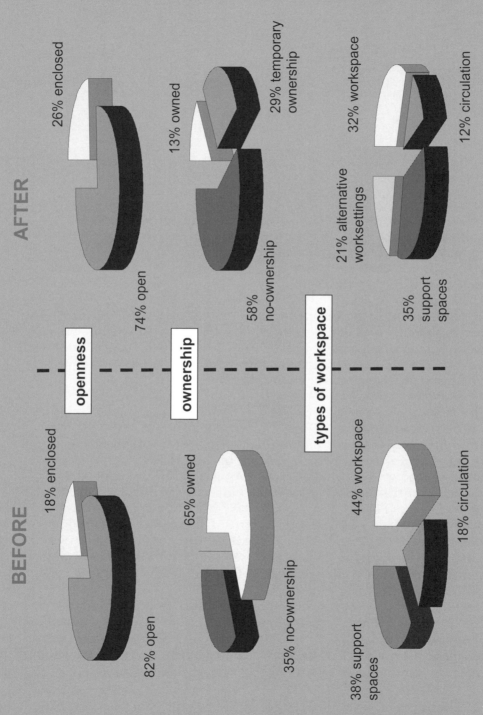

Figure 2.1   Analysis of key spatial characteristics before and after office re-design, DEGW

Source: DEGW/Bell.

Whilst seemingly bucking the perceived 'make everywhere open-plan' trend, the DEGW transition at this time was indicative of the growing recognition of the need for a range of shared and dedicated worksettings, as well as open and enclosed (or semi-enclosed) spaces, to support the diverse and dynamic nature of modern office work. The desk had become no longer the best place to do everything. Not all meetings needed to take place in formal, enclosed surroundings. Places to do quiet, concentrative or confidential work, away from the desk, were now required. Important informal, spontaneous interaction also needed to be supported. Some staff were in the office more than others, with some literally dropping in for short times only for meetings or to catch up on e-mails. Project and cross-team working, along with the sharing of knowledge and ideas, was becoming much more important and needed to be encouraged and facilitated. All in all, a different kind of workplace was required and was emerging – the 'landscaped office' – so-called because of its rich and interesting variety of worksettings.

This provided a much needed breath of fresh air for office design and a new challenge for those involved in their creation. It also presented new opportunities to provide a more functional office environment where staff could match tasks to the optimum worksetting and thus be more effective.

It is worth emphasising that such workplaces would still seek to provide generic solutions for organisations, which are applicable across various teams. Generic solutions do not have to be limited and boring. And the need to avoid the unnecessary cost of creating inflexible, over-personalised workspace was, and still is, as strong as ever.

A whole new language of trendy worksetting terminology arose as part of this office 'landscaping' development: examples being touchdowns (for short-stay working), pods and study booths (for concentrative work), chill-out rooms, lounges (for quieter, more reflective

> **'...a different kind of workplace was required and was emerging – the "landscaped office"...'**

work), hubs and resource areas (for printing, copying, shredding and so on), hot-desk and hot-offices (shared workspace available on an ad-hoc or bookable basis) and club, breakout and cafe areas (for relaxed interaction).

The latter was a reflection that, at last, the coffee culture that was becoming so popular for work and leisure outside the office, could now be re-created *inside* the office – and retain the important 'cafe' buzz and energy within the organisation. And very popular it was. Staff, with the support of more flexible technology and changing work practices and attitudes, deserted their desks to take full advantage of these new settings. Work became more sociable, more interesting and, with the right personal disciplines, more effective. Project progress, key decision making and one-to-one liaisons, previously delayed by meeting room bottlenecks, was made easier and more attractive by spontaneous informal interaction (and often with the benefit of good coffee!).

Getting it right

Many organisations will today likely operate in the more sophisticated, multi-worksetting-based 'landscaped' work environments along the lines just described – which have the potential to be much more fit-for-purpose and effective than previous, more traditional working environments. But *potential* is the key word – as it is not easy to always get it right, or get it right first time. Some such new workplaces may be less effective than desired or intended. There are a number of factors affecting this.

> **'Technology is especially important, but so also is workplace management and protocols.'**

One is that the organisational culture needs to be appropriately aligned with the workplace created. People will not leave their desks and either disappear into quieter areas or be seen frequenting coffee bars if there is a culture of 'presenteeism' linked to

the desk (that is, if you are not at your desk, you are not working). Leadership by example is required to re-affirm that new work patterns and behaviours are acceptable and desired. The workforce also needs to be 'educated', through well-planned change management processes, to understand how to make best use of the new options and opportunities with confidence.

Another factor is having the right infrastructure to support this new diverse and dynamic work environment. Technology is especially important, but so also is workplace management and protocols. Again people will not leave their desks and desktop technology for alternative worksettings if they don't have the means to take their work with them – either through portable devices, ideally with wireless capability or through 'log on anywhere' facilities with roaming profiles.[2] People will also not use shared worksettings if they are messy or cluttered or appear to be in use or 'owned' by someone else. Booking and clearing-up protocols are all-important here, ideally managed and re-enforced through a concierge-style office-management role.

Finally, the actual design and layout of this new style of working environment is absolutely key to its effectiveness. As any chef would know, the output of using a recognised menu of ingredients, in this case the new alternative worksetting options, is only as good as the way they are put together and applied, and in the workplace context this is indeed a skilled task. Careful thought around the workplace dynamics are required to understand the balance and the configuration of worksettings required, linked to the anticipated workstyles of its occupants. For example, the degree of open versus enclosed space, formal versus informal space, owned versus shared space; as well as how many desks versus study areas versus touchdown spaces versus breakout space versus offices, and so on.

---

2   Roaming profiles – where your personal PC desktop set up is re-created at whatever location and machine you log into within the office environment.

In addition, the positioning of these elements within the workspace is critical to ensure that the different work modes, activities and movements of staff can be accommodated without causing distraction or conflict. For example, positioning touchdowns and meeting rooms near main circulation and entrances to workspace to avoid unnecessary disturbance to other workers; or positioning hub, breakout or cafe areas in obvious circulation centres, so their attraction and use will be natural, but they are also not too close to workspace so as to cause distractions. Also, perhaps most obvious of all, ensuring quieter areas are positioned away from noisier, more interactive workspace. This all sounds like common sense, but so often workspace is planned on a best-fit basis, without proper consideration to how it will be used and the implications of dynamic use. See illustrative examples of landscaped office worksetting arrangements – Figures 2.2 and 2.3(a and b).

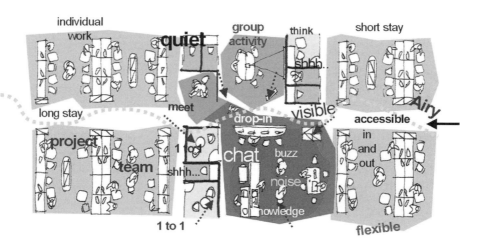

Figure 2.2   Landscaped office illustration – layout characteristics
Source: DEGW.

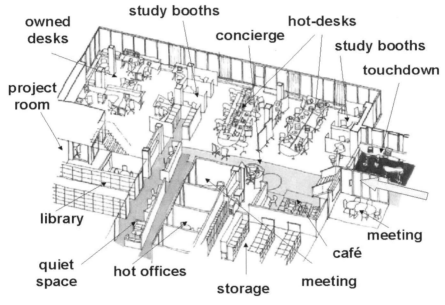

Figure 2.3a   Landscaped office illustrations – worksettings in context
Source: DEGW/Bell.

Design characteristics can also make a difference in terms of the performance, comfort and attraction of new worksettings. The amount of space, the comfort of chairs, the ease of adaption for different users, the use of sound-absorbing materials, even the quality of coffee all contribute to the effectiveness of these settings.

I have seen many a post-occupancy study that has revealed that certain new worksettings, deemed as necessary, are found to be unpopular and little used. Over-provision and incorrect positioning are often factors here. The reality is that you cannot always get it right in advance. The design of such workspace

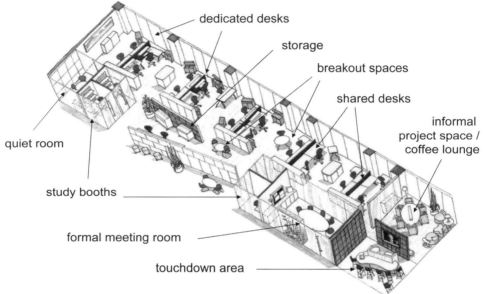

Figure 2.3b   Landscaped office illustrations – worksettings in context
Source: DEGW/Bell.

needs to be linked to an advance 'briefing' process to understand the business and user requirements involved, including future needs and aspirations. However, even then, often the take-up and use of such new work environments provide some unexpected outcomes and patterns of use. Thus the discipline of appropriate post-occupancy reviews (informal and formal) and ability to respond to such reviews and refine the work environment are very important.

Back to the desk

I started this chapter by referring to the aim of both creating an efficient and effective working environment. The drive towards providing staff with

a choice and range of office worksettings to improve their effectiveness is admirable. However, often this involves the provision of additional, new facilities that potentially requires additional space. This can, of course, have the impact of reducing the efficiency of the workspace to the extent that desired improvements may not even be viable. The approach here has to be that the greater degree of alternative worksettings provided or desired, the less traditional worksettings – that is, dedicated desks and formal meeting rooms – you need to provide. After all, staff cannot be in two places at once when they are in the office workplace.

This quite logically implies consideration of desk-sharing, as part of the process of introducing supplementary, alternative worksettings. Aside from the inefficiencies, not to do so can also leave workspaces half-empty. They will become quieter as a result, probably too quiet – where every small noise becomes an exaggerated distraction and the space becomes lifeless and without the desired buzz and energy of a successful office environment.

It is interesting that, even when there are minimal alternative worksettings to draw people away from their desks, the simple transformation to a more open, and thus more visible, working environment can often in itself reveal unexpected levels of desk under-utilisation; reflecting factors like meetings, work in other locations and staff absence through sickness, holidays and training. This can be measured more specifically through the undertaking of space utilisation studies, which formally track the use and utilisation of space over a period of time, typically a fortnight. Figure 2.4 provides two illustrative outputs from such an exercise.

> '...the office desk is often simply a convenient base for people to use sporadically while they are in the office.'

The reality is that many office workers today are knowledge-workers and networkers, typically spending much of their time in formal and

Daily activity pattern — across all workspace (desks)

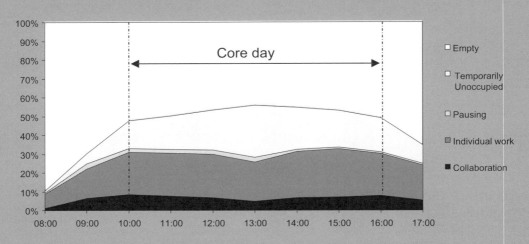
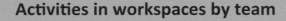

Profile of activities across all desks across working day — shows daily trend of utilisation
Note: Unoccupied (temporarily) indicates someone is in the office but not at their desk

Activities in workspaces by team

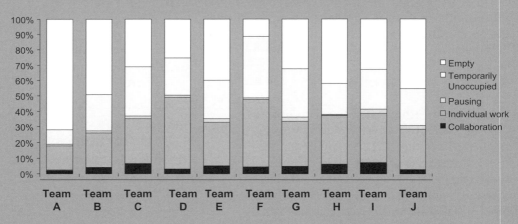

Breakdown by team, shows the variant patterns of utilisation across teams

Figure 2.4   Illustrative outputs from a space utlisation study
Source: DEGW/Bell.

informal meetings, as well as being involved in multi-project work. They also increasingly spend a portion of their working days in other locations, including home. In these circumstances, the office desk is often simply a convenient base for people to use sporadically while they are in the office.

Desk-sharing and the 'new deal'

So if we want to ensure that re-designing the office into a 'landscaped office' does not compromise the efficiency of the space or its ability to create the right atmosphere, desk-sharing has to be considered. In addition, the very nature of people's jobs and workstyles are also increasingly reflecting less dependency on the office desk. Figure 2.5 outlines the characteristics of the most typical emerging workstyles. There will always be the odd role that perhaps suggests a variation or even addition to these generic examples – for example, counter clerks or real technical specialist; but generally speaking, there is only ever around six or so workstyles in any organisation. This figure also highlights where the potential for desk-sharing is most appropriate. See where you or your team fit into this model!

Introducing desk-sharing will never be easy. As mentioned in the introduction to this book, the desk has become the last stable refuge for staff in the turbulent world of work and organisational change. Instinctively people will want to hold on to this provision, often viewed as an entitlement. But as significant as this desire may be, the desk also holds the key for the flexibility that will be essential for the future – for both the workplace and the office-worker. For many, it is now time to let go!

Use of pilots can be useful to support the introduction of desk-sharing, to demonstrate how – with a well-designed, well-managed and suitably technology-enabled new working environment – working without a dedicated desk can be extremely effective and liberating. I personally have not had a dedicated desk now for some 15 years or dedicated storage for

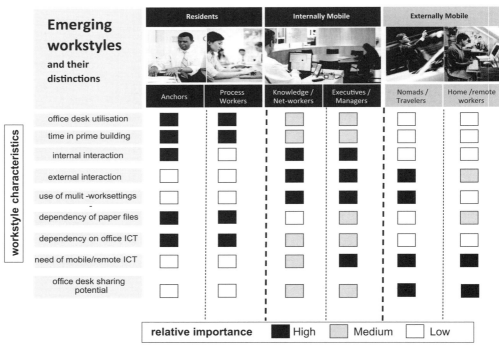

Emerging workstyles and their distinctions	Residents		Internally Mobile		Externally Mobile	
workstyle characteristics	Anchors	Process Workers	Knowledge / Net-workers	Executives / Managers	Nomads / Travelers	Home /remote workers
office desk utilisation	High	High	Medium	Medium	Low	Low
time in prime building	High	High	Medium	Medium	Low	Low
internal interaction	High	Low	High	High	Low	Low
external interaction	Low	Low	High	High	High	Medium
use of mulit -worksettings	Low	Low	High	High	High	Low
dependency of paper files	High	High	Low	Low	Low	Medium
dependency on office ICT	High	High	Medium	Medium	Low	Low
need of mobile/remote ICT	Low	Low	Medium	High	High	High
office desk sharing potential	Low	Low	Medium	Medium	High	High

relative importance ■ High ▨ Medium □ Low

Figure 2.5   Characteristics of emerging generic workstyles
Source: DEGW/Bell.

7 years. I value other things more, like good technology and the ability to follow a flexible workstyle that meets mutual needs. It is this sort of 'new deal' that has to be part of the incentive for workers to make this important transition.

Like so many other workplace initiatives, early implementations of desk-sharing (hot-desking or hotelling being the popular terms then) were crude

and thus unpopular – with staff feeling they had lost out, rather than gained anything new. 'Second class citizens' is how someone once put it to me.

Desk-sharing, as an integral part of introducing a new dynamic multi-worksetting environment, needs to be well thought-through and implemented sensitively. But with the potential efficiencies available, there is no reason why proper investment can't be made to ensure the resultant workplace is a more attractive and effective place to be – and this will make its occupants feel special.

One of the oft-cited criticisms of efficient open workspaces based on 1:1 desking (a dedicated desk per person) is that they are often manifested by very predictable, linear workplace, with rows of desks in lines – like battery hens or a classroom, I have heard some describe it, perhaps a little unfairly. Truth is that such a layout is probably the optimum and most efficient way of planning the workspace and the number of workstations required. Clearly, with some creativity in the space planning and design features, the workspace should be able to be made more appealing – but there will be limits, particularly if the expectation is that the workspace has to accommodate desired alternative worksettings as well.

> **'Introducing desk-sharing will never be easy.'**

On the contrary, with desk-sharing there is the scope to both introduce further alternative worksettings and, in doing so, provide a more interesting and relaxed workplace layout – and save space as well. Such is the impact of moving away from a 1:1 desking arrangement.

It is worth emphasising that desk-sharing should not now just be confined to teams who are 'out and about' a lot – sales teams, consultants, inspectors and the like. Knowledge-workers typically have very mobile workstyles within the office and are often in formal and informal meetings (as the earlier

Figure 2.5 indicated) and thus are prime candidates for desk-sharing. Public counter staff are good examples of those that probably share well already, but 'back-office' arrangements may still warrant review. Incidentally, staff making use of unopened counter points to do 'back office' work can present a very frustrating sight for queuing customers, so good screening is ideal here to enable more comfortable working!

> '...rows of desks in lines
> – like battery hens or a
> classroom...'

I worked with a knowledge-based public sector organisation sometime back who introduced desk-sharing across the majority of the organisation as part of a planned office move. This was not because staff were away from the office, but because they were so internally mobile. The initiative was aptly named 'free-desking', which had much more positive connotations that 'hot-desking'.

Interestingly, staff completed pre-move questionnaires about their workstyles and were actually asked whether, taking into account the nature of their work and the facilities the new building would provide, they required a dedicated desk in the new office. Amazingly, just under half of respondents felt they didn't need a dedicated desk and this gave the organisation the confidence to progress with its initiative. Sometimes it is worth being as blunt, open and straightforward as this on such matters; although I think the overall manner in which staff were positively prepared for this particular office move was exceptionally good. Not just down to me, but enlightened senior management!

Sharing in phases

On another occasion I worked on a major relocation project for a media organisation that, quite rightly, introduced a range of additional new worksettings to support its very dynamic and creative workforce. However,

they were unable to persuade (or prepared to force) their staff to 'give up' their dedicated desks. Consequently, their new office workplace was a mixed success, with valued new worksettings being well used to the detriment of the main desk areas which were soul-less and visibly very wasteful. They are now addressing this, because the issue was so open and obvious. And perhaps this was a natural two-stage process that was necessary culturally.

The positive thing is that this workplace was designed, particularly in terms of its furniture solutions, to adapt very easily to desk-sharing arrangements. The desks were bench-style with no under-desk pedestals for personal storage (as this was in nearby individually-lockable drawers), so the physical transition was easy. The cultural transition will take a little longer of course. But this highlights the importance of both tackling radical cultural change in sensible phases and future-proofing the office design.

Different strokes

There are different desk-sharing models of course, which adds to the scope and opportunity here – both in terms of the sharing ratios and arrangements for who gets involved. In terms of ratios, 8:10 (8 desks for every 10 people) or 7:10 (7 desks for every 10 people) are the most popular – but in some cases sharing ratios can be pushed harder for more impact – 1:3 or 1:2 (1 desk for every 3 or 2 people) is a popular model for more mobile consulting organisations. The higher the degree of sharing, the more opportunities there are for efficiencies and creating a more interesting workplace; and often the difference between ratios in terms of negative apprehension for staff is minimal. The biggest cultural hurdle is introducing the concept of sharing in the first instance. Once you can get past this, you can of course play around with different sharing ratios – that is,

> '...the importance of both tackling radical cultural change in sensible phases and future-proofing the office design.'

start off gently and then increase until a challenging, but comfortable level is reached.

The more interesting, variable aspect of desk-sharing is around who gets involved. Traditionally the approach has been to identify the most obvious candidates – those perhaps out of the office most – and insist that they share, whilst others retain dedicated desks. However, this may have a negative impact in terms of numbers involved, potentially creating an 'us and them' situation and failing to achieve the economies of scale to enable a sensible sharing ratio and decent shared work environment (with the ideal associated alternative worksettings). This situation is often aggravated further when desk-sharers note that their so-called desk-bound colleagues are hardly at their desks either, causing understandable resentment. This has happened on a number of times on projects I have been involved in.

A more satisfactory model is to get the majority of, or indeed all, staff involved – thus making it an inclusive process. In this way, scale enables a more appropriate workplace to be created and avoids a two-tier workforce.

With all this flexibility and liberation, staff still appreciate a sense of belonging and allowing teams to come together with ease will be important. The creation of team zones within the building or floorplate (defined areas but not with rigid boundaries) where staff can naturally come together to work with their team colleagues (if they want to), are recommended here. In such models, sometimes key people like secretaries may still have a dedicated base, as 'anchors' to teams. But even if everybody participates in the desk-sharing, inevitably some staff will likely come in and sit in the same (favourite) place most days, if they are in; but this is OK. Others may choose to move around a space or even a building to a much higher degree. It is all about choice.

But the principle that space isn't 'owned' and can be used by others if it is unoccupied is the important element. This provides the desired efficiencies and opportunities to create a more interesting, dynamic and effective working environment. A clear desk policy, that is, clearing away all papers and personal effects after use will, of course, be imperative as part of new workplace protocols to ensure sharing workspace can operate effectively. I will touch more on new workplace protocols in the next chapter.

And there's more...

Desk-sharing of course is only one, perhaps very topical and emotive, element of workplace change that is required to exploit the opportunities around creating a more efficient and effective workplace. There will be many others, such as storage reduction, reduced use of paper, implementation and adoption of new technologies, revised work processes and procedures and, most importantly, the cultural changes, inspired by enlightened leadership, that will determine the true take-up and acceptance of workplace changes and ensure ultimate, sustainable success. I will explore the cultural challenges and opportunities around staff engagement further in my next chapter.

Technology is also, of course, essential to workplace effectiveness. Without the appropriate harnessing of technology by an organisation, much of the assumed workplace and work practice developments are hampered, even impossible. Technology is critical to the mobility of work that is so important now, both within and beyond the office; and this in itself is contributing to perhaps the biggest factor to impact the future office workplace – the divergence of work and place and the advent of distributed working.

I will explore further the impact of technology and distributed working in the later, very significant, e-work chapter. However, suffice to say that the developments and future expectations explored in that chapter throw completely new challenges to the workplace – positioning the effectiveness considerations discussed in this chapter into a totally new context. Such developments will further reinforce the need for alternative worksettings, especially those that bring people together to interact and work collaboratively; as well as the need for increased sharing of resources and, most importantly, to break the time-bound personal tie to the desk.

Furthermore, the expected expansion of work and place opportunities will see many workers naturally breaking ties with the office workplace itself. For many staff the office workplace will just be one of a number of choices and options available to them for work – and not necessarily the default as is now. Work will no longer be where you go, but what you do. And increasingly work can be done in any place and at any time. By effectively distributing work across the city and rural landscapes in this way, new opportunities for work/life balance, local economies, commuting patterns, customer service and organisational effectiveness are possible. A potential 'win-win-win-win' for organisations, their workforce, their customers and their community, is possible, if you can get it right.

> **'Without the appropriate harnessing of technology by an organisation, much of the assumed workplace and work practice developments are hampered, even impossible.'**

In this broader context, the role and effectiveness of the office workplace takes on a whole new meaning and its ability to compete and be attractive, as a destination of choice, will be all-important. The image of the office and the experience of working there is under the microscope like never before. But this is a challenge the office workplace can win.

Much of what is suggested in this chapter as innovation will prove to be a necessity. A no-brainer. In many respects, the move to the more effective dynamic, landscaped office and re-assessment of the role and use of the desk is simply the stepping stone to the future – but a critical step that must be understood, embraced and taken boldly.

Engagement

The previous chapters have explored a number of ways in which the workplace can become more efficient and effective. Most of this implied both physical, as well as, importantly, cultural change – that is, a change to the 'way things are done', embracing both procedural and behavioural considerations. In many respects, true workplace effectiveness can only be achieved through such people factors.

3 Engagement

People power

The previous chapters have explored a number of ways in which the workplace can become more efficient and effective. Most of this implied both physical, as well as, importantly, cultural change – that is, a change to the 'way things are done', embracing both procedural and behavioural considerations. In many respects, true workplace effectiveness can only be achieved through such people factors.

One of the most common expressions I have used in my consulting work is that 'people are the most important workplace ingredient'. And how true this is when you think about it. 'People are the key to your success, or the reason for your failure' is another phrase I use. It is clear that if you want to achieve successful workplace transformations, you also need to be good at 'people' and 'change'. Workplace change is an emotive area, as we have already discussed, and thus needs to be handled with care. But people are powerful, so you want to harness their positive energy at all times.

Even where the most appropriate workplace solution is developed and there are no compromises in the money spent or quality achieved, such a workplace is totally dependent on its workforce occupants – that is, the people – to be successful. The new investments made are worthless without the understanding, acceptance and commitment of people. Staff trying to work in 'old ways' in a new-style working environment can be disastrous. Indeed, without the necessary mindset change, the solution may be undermined by resistance and negative energy that will prevent or diminish intended outcomes. In these circumstances, superficial physical change is all that can be achieved.

> '..."people are the most important workplace ingredient".'

The flipside of this is equally important; if you are trying to affect cultural, process or organisational change without making any changes to the working environment, you are ignoring, as I pointed out at the end of Chapter 1, perhaps your most powerful change tool – the working environment – and thus missing important opportunities. Even worse, without either effective cultural or workplace change, the impact of any initiative is going to be very limited indeed. See Figure 3.1 opposite.

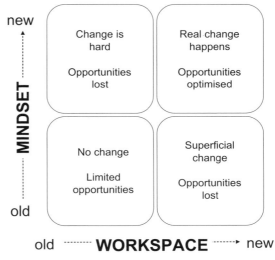

Figure 3.1   **Dynamics between mindset change and workplace change**

Source: Bell.

Psychology in the workplace

At a very simplistic level, there are a couple of principles of psychology that come into play here.

One is the use of strong, credible leadership – where those who are influential (who are not always the most senior people, of course) support the changes and embrace them by example and action. For a whole range of reasons, not least peer and career pressures, this influence will rub off on others who will want to align themselves with such leadership. There will also be important confidence in the change process created in these circumstances.

By appropriately involving and harnessing positive leadership and engaging with influential resistors – for example, using the more enlightened as 'sponsors' and 'champions' – you can more effectively focus your change efforts on the most influential people as the route to engaging the wider workforce indirectly. See Figure 3.2.

The second principle is around developing ownership of the changes, linked to personal benefits and kudos. As anyone who has tried to convince a loved one to embrace a desired change which they are resisting has discovered, an effective strategy is to make them feel like it was their idea, which naturally they will then want to pursue and support. Perhaps not quite as crudely as this, but helping people understand 'what's in it for them' and involving them in the change process can help achieve this important ownership and personal commitment, which otherwise would not exist. User groups, staff workshops, staff task teams and team discussion and team-based action-planning can all support this cause.

Linked to creating this 'sense of ownership' is the desire for us all to need some logic, reason or rationale to move from one state to another. Just think about our personal lives – we embrace change all the time, some of it easier than others – but as long as there is sufficient reasoning and motivation, we will embrace change, even if it means compromise or some initial discomfort.

> **'...helping people understand "what's in it for them"...'**

Moving house is a good example here, or changing job, car or child's school. In the workplace change context this rationale and motivation might exist at a personal, team and/or organisational level, and even where the rationale is fairly hard and blunt – linked perhaps to cost cutting and organisational survival – it is much better to be open about this, as staff will get wind of things anyway and don't like having the 'wool pulled over their eyes'!

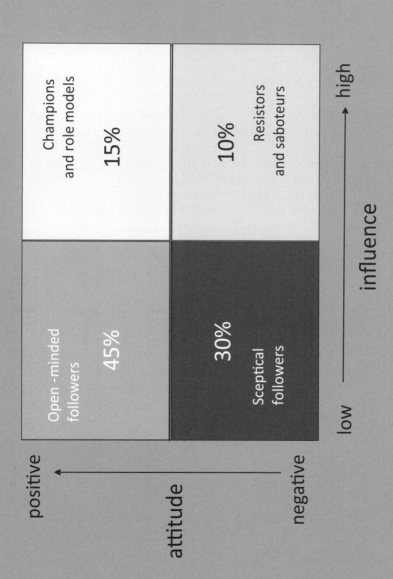

positive

attitude

negative

Open-minded
followers

45%

Sceptical
followers

30%

Champions
and role models

15%

10%

Resistors
and saboteurs

low

influence

high

- Percentages show typically how an organisation may be identified and split
- Focusing on 25% of the organisation can strongly influence change; 75% may follow
- 15% nurtured as champions; 10% to be positively managed and guided
- Managing negativity should not represent more than 40% of the effort

Figure 3.2 **Workforce analyis – influence and positivity matrix**
Source: Bell.

Multi-methods and media

As a general rule, open, clear, timely and relevant communication is imperative to effective staff engagement. We often delay communication (and decision making) when there is difficult news or uncertainty; however the void is quickly filled by speculation and rumour, which can make the situation even worse and negatively impact project credibility. A well-researched communication strategy and plan (and associated stakeholder analysis to understand your different audiences) is a vital element for any successful workplace change project. A range of media and mechanisms can, and should, be used to support planned activities. In this way, a spectrum of staff preferences can be accommodated, maximising the inclusiveness of the engagement process.

I don't know if you have ever had the experience of making a sales pitch or attending an interview and realising, when it didn't go well, that in hindsight your choice of style of presentation and material was wrong. Though perhaps perfect and successful on a previous occasion with someone else, it just didn't work on that occasion. This is a simple personality-style mismatch – and it can happen in the context of workplace change communications too. Some people need to see facts and figures before they embrace change; some need to see 'proof'; some need to be seduced by the excitement of the change or the personal benefits available ('what's in it for me?'). Some people only accept change if everybody else is happy. There are a number of ways you can respond to all these needs by using different media, different types of material and different engagement processes (like user groups or committees). Not everybody is the same and your communications cannot afford to alienate anyone.

> **'We often delay communication (and decision making) when there is difficult news or uncertainty...'**

There is also a thin line to tread between educating and patronising staff when dealing with the introduction of new workplace

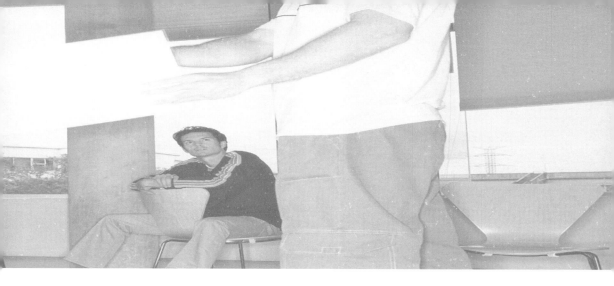

concepts, so another important factor, and equally applicable to the pitch or interview scenario previously described, is doing your 'homework'. By this I mean undertaking necessary early research and assessment of the organisation and the 'mood' of staff. Diagnostics I call it. In the same way as a doctor examines a patient before prescribing medicine; so an assessment process should be made to inform your workplace change management approach and tactics. 'Change readiness' questionnaires can be helpful here. Even just being aware of how past change projects have gone can give you some important clues.

Friend and foe

I remember during one project finding myself in danger of being subsumed in managing the negative resistance from a small, but very vocal and influential, minority – and structuring my whole change strategy around them. I realised that I was neglecting the more positive, or at least neutral and persuadable, majority, so deliberately set out to address this imbalance and assume a more positive basis for project

> 'Not everybody is the same and your communications cannot afford to alienate anyone.'

communications and interventions. This was important as I was then able to generate a positive groundswell which created compelling peer pressure to draw in others. I did, nevertheless, still spend time with one or two senior negative individuals who did eventually become much more supportive – and, given their previous stance, eventually became extremely powerful ambassadors for the project. Essentially, once people saw such serial cynics become convinced, they were more confident and comfortable about 'buying in' themselves.

Interestingly, the enlightenment for the negative influencers in question came after, not before, implementation; reminding us that some people do need to see evidence and experience things first hand before they will take on new

ideas. It also reminds us that different people move along the recognised stages of change or 'change curve' at different paces and all this needs to be reflected in an effective and responsive change management programme that works with the communication strategy and its range of media and methods. Such a programme should effectively reflect the stages or journey of change; but also allow people to absorb and reflect on change at a pace that works for them.

Change management model

This experience also serves to reinforce the point that the post-change period, when people are settling in and adapting in the new working environment, is absolutely critical to the embedding of change. Figure 3.3 outlines the key phases from a typical workplace change management project, including the post-change embedding and review phase. Each phase in this model will typically incorporate a range of activities and interventions relevant to the stage of the project.

For example, senior envisioning and organisational culture assessment activities might feature in the first phase, as well as project set-up to effectively kick the programme off.

Staff presentations and the launch of an intranet and/or e-bulletins might feature as part of the 'awareness-raising' second phase.

Figure 3.3   Five workplace change management phases
Source: Bell.

The third phase may be spread over a considerable period of time and might include staff workshops and task team activities (to explore and develop areas such as new protocols development, storage reduction, new technologies and new work practices), or even a pilot or mock-up to support the preparation and adjustment process.

The fourth phase would typically include practically-focused guidance on the new workspace, move-related instructions, familiarisation visits and move-in support and training.

The final phase deals with the important embedding of change and review of 'how things are going', including any formal post-occupancy evaluations. Ideally attention to the ongoing monitoring, management and development of the workplace should be a permanent process and securing resources for this is a critical step that ideally needs to be made for any organisation.

This latter point reflects the desirable viewpoint that the workplace is a key strategic enabler for the business and needs to be constantly managed and evolved to ensure it is optimised – in a similar way to how we now take a much more strategic view on how we invest in and, *importantly*, refresh our technologies. Change and development, in every sense, is a constant. A workplace change champion should similarly be a permanent role.

New ways of consulting

As is probably now quite clear, engagement or consultation with staff cannot be as it was in the past. It is no longer appropriate to seek or encourage a wish-list of requirements; as these are likely to be based around existing arrangements which may no longer apply. The consultation process needs to

focus on understanding the nature of current and future business needs and aspirations and challenging conventional thinking where necessary; asking people what they do or will do (to deliver their business) rather than what they want. This is a much more appropriate way of 'briefing' requirements for a new workplace.

Solutions need to be based on objective analysis of this 'demand', which is then assessed in the context of the physical workplace buildings or other 'place' options that are available as 'supply'. In this way, solutions are not immediately constrained by predetermined physical solutions. Choices for staff will still be there, but they will be more around how people work and use the new workspace – that is, their workstyles – rather than them getting too involved in the detailed design of the new physical workplace.

The focus also has to be on helping staff to understand the rationale behind the new approach and positively helping them to embrace the solutions, as it is a significant shift away from more traditional expectations around staff consultation and engagement. A way I have described this recently is to suggest that staff 'don't necessarily get what they want, but they do want what they get; and importantly they understand, accept and embrace the differences'.[1]

If all this sounds a bit directive, it is; because if the fundamental changes needed are to be achieved, it needs to be properly led and directed. However, change management in this context has come a long way from its origins, where people were regarded as obstacles to initiatives that had to be 'managed' or overcome; nowadays a more involved and inclusive process

> **'Organisations need talented people more than talented people need organisations...'**

---

1   Quotation from 'Working beyond walls' – DEGW/OGC publication July 2008.

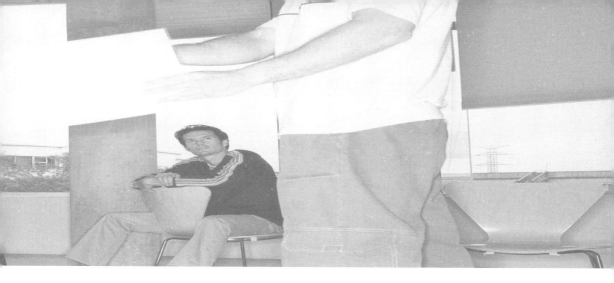

is required and expected, where the true requirements are professionally determined, solutions sensitively explained and expectations suitably managed.

Talent spotting

There may appear to be some conflict here, in that we are continually being reminded how precious staff with the right skills are; how organisations must do everything they can to attract and retain the right people or 'talent' as it is often called. Organisations need talented people more than talented people need organisations[2] is one way I have heard it summed up. You could therefore argue that, in this context, the organisation should provide whatever workplace the employee requires, to keep them happy as it were, and no doubt some staff will still push for this.

But, perhaps more positively, there is a natural alignment between the sort of 'talent' that is so sought after and the new and evolving approach to the workplace. There is no doubt that the growth in knowledge worker roles and jobs (which require often complex interactions needing high levels of judgement) far exceeds that of more transitional jobs (which require more routine interactions and processes that can be easily automated or scripted) – and it is these 'growth' roles that benefit most from the workplace developments that are emerging. It is these workers who will insist in the ability to work flexibly across time and location. Indeed, such workplace arrangements will help create a culture that both attracts and fosters such employees.

I am also minded to think about my children who are just starting to enter the workplace as part of the next generation workforce. We need to design workplaces for them as much as ourselves. They will be tomorrow's knowledge-

---

2   Daniel Pink – Free Agent Nation – 2001.

workers and decision makers, talent even, and they will not tolerate many aspects of the old order, but rather insist on fit-for-purpose, stimulating and dynamic places to do their work.

Best behaviour

Just to finish off this chapter on the human aspect of workplace change, it is worth mentioning the need to establish and enforce the concept of new workplace protocols to enable harmonious working in the new, dynamic workplaces and workstyles being suggested. All offices have some form of behavioural code or etiquette, often referred to as protocols. It may not be written down, as it has often become established over a number of years, but it is usually well understood nevertheless. A new style of working environment – where perhaps staff are in a more open environment than before or are embarking on a greater level of sharing resources or mobility – will call on the need to re-visit the office protocols, to avoid conflict and discomfort. Examples here might be around noise and distractions, eating, security, cleanliness and clearing up, use of telephones, desk personalisation, even music in the office.

What people may have done previously in their own office may not be acceptable in a more open environment. If workspaces are to be shared, they need to be left as you would expect to find them. Most of this is based upon common sense and courtesy; and a generic set of new protocols is something that can quickly be sourced[3] or developed, often based on what other organisations have done and best practice.

However, it is important that staff do not see such a behaviour code as imposed rules. Ideally staff should get involved in developing these protocols, perhaps as a means of working through anticipated issues and

3   Reference – Working without walls – DEGW/OGC publication 2004, pages 35 and 41.

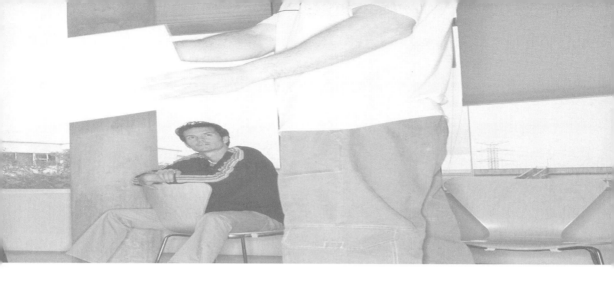

concerns (as protocols can usually address many of these) through workshop activities, for example. In this way, there will be the desired 'ownership' that will help the protocols to be properly embraced and put into everyday practice. Often developed ahead of a workplace change, the protocols do need to be reviewed over time to ensure they are still relevant and appropriate. Experience may reveal the need for additional protocols, not anticipated, for example.

> **'What people may have done previously in their own office may not be acceptable in a more open environment.'**

Many of the new protocols needed in the future may, of course, have little to do with the office at all – but more about our interaction with it. For example, how and when distributed workers come together as teams; how often you check into the office; how you signal when you are available online or not; how you keep your manager updated on work matters when you rarely see him or her; how you ensure organisational data is not compromised when working in public places; and probably most important of all, how you keep the discipline of sensibly 'logging off' from work when working at home.

Bed-mail

To illustrate the latter example, I am sure you have had, at some point, e-mails from colleagues at 2:00 am in the morning. You may even have sent e-mail at such times yourselves. Nothing wrong with this, I guess, if your body clock is at its best at that time of day – just as long as you remember to have a lie-in bed in the morning.

Figure 3.4 shows a drawing my eldest son drew at school when he was 9 years old, a period when I was extensively working from home and keen to prove to my employer that it could work. The image portrays, when you note

Figure 3.4   Child eye view of flexible working (child's drawing)
Source: Bell.

the clock (almost 6:00 am?) and my dishevelled state, that I was probably overdoing things a bit at that time. I have since learnt, through experience, to manage my work and personal time much better.

At the time, I recall my son also expressed a strong desire 'to do what daddy does' for a living when he grew up. I don't think it was the long hours or stress levels that were attractive to him – clearly I was able to adequately

hide that from the family – but it was the idea of being able to play with 'cool' technology (not by today's standards of course) and lie in bed all day which seemed such an idyllic occupation. Interestingly, he now works in IT, rolling out flexible work solutions for a major retail organisation. What goes around comes around, so they say.

Expression

Early chapters in this book track the fairly well-recognised areas of understanding and optimising workplace performance by looking at efficiency and effectiveness factors. However in more recent years a new measure and additional 'e' factor has come to the fore in this context – 'expression'. A further balancing influence to the perhaps 'harder' drivers of efficiency and effectiveness; and interestingly an aspect that can sometimes 'overrule' the other two drivers in order to be allowed to optimise its impact. It can also play its part in supporting the staff engagement process just discussed – by helping to make the new order an attractive, exciting and relevant proposition.

4 Expression

Communication through physical form

Early chapters in this book track the fairly well-recognised areas of understanding and optimising workplace performance by looking at efficiency and effectiveness factors. However, in more recent years a new measure and additional 'e' factor has come to the fore in this context – 'expression'. A further balancing influence to the perhaps 'harder' drivers of efficiency and effectiveness; and interestingly an aspect that can sometimes 'overrule' the other two drivers in order to be allowed to optimise its impact. It can also play its part in supporting the staff engagement process just discussed – by helping to make the new order an attractive, exciting and relevant proposition.

The 'expression' term is something I first heard muted in my time with international workplace consultants DEGW back in the late 1990s. However, it was only to become a more 'public' idea through the later 2005 collaborative research publication 'The impact of office design on business performance'.[1]

Essentially in this context, 'expression' relates to the messages that the physical environment sends to its occupants, users and visitors. These messages may be subtle or they may be purposely 'in your face'; much depending on the desired outcome of such communication. Typically the purpose of the message would be to inform and influence in some way and often to re-enforce organisational or product branding; or organisational values and culture. In this way, such 'expression' can play a significant influencing role in supporting organisational change, adding further to the impact of workplace change as a catalyst.

There is a strong commercial reality about this form of expression too, which the modern-day workplace has been largely slow to fully understand

---

1   DEGW, Commission for Architecture and the Built Environment (CABE) and British Council of Offices (BCO) joint research project and report, 2005.

and exploit. Whether wowing customers or motivating or attracting new staff, the power of expression, particularly through clever and creative design and imagery, is undeniable. This is something that the retail industry has exploited for years. Originally focusing on external 'window dressing' and branding, expression now shouts out throughout such retail stores through suggestive displays, imagery and clever lighting – to draw us in and encourage sales. Ditto hotels, restaurants and clubs.

Using building form to make a statement is nothing new, of course, but it has lost its way somewhat in more recent times. The skyscrapers of New York, Chicago and countless other cities around the world sought to impress and symbolise a successful, dominating organisation. The grandeur of Government buildings in Whitehall (London), spoke of the power and glory of times when their occupants helped rule a British Empire. Even inside any of these buildings, impressive entrances and lavish hospitality facilities continued the story. Such expression created its own competition for the largest, tallest or most opulent.

Even today, the provision of buildings to express success, size and quality of service or product still feature; although there have been some significant shifts in recent times and a greater emphasis placed on the interior of buildings.

Most skyscrapers and tower blocks today are now multi-occupied and thus fairly anonymous from the outside, driven in part by cost and business dispersal. So organisations need to use their interiors and their 'front door' receptions to make their statements. In the most recent times of terrorism and security threat, this lower external profile is becoming a necessity for

> **'Whether wowing customers or motivating or attracting new staff, the power of expression, particularly through clever and creative design and imagery, is undeniable.'**

many. In this sense, the days of statement buildings and huge corporate neon may be truly gone.

Another phenomenon worth touching on was the 1960s and 1970s drive to quickly produce hundreds of bland (post-modernism) functional-style office blocks. Here expression was still at play, but it was deliberately about crude function and efficiency – almost as a correction to the perceived extravagance of the past. The expansion of Government in London from Whitehall into the numerous office blocks in Victoria about this time is testimony to this shift of style and emphasis.

However, the expression misfired in that these buildings actually became the symbolism of dull bureaucracy and inefficiency, which the Civil Service is still trying to live down today. Most of these buildings are now thankfully being demolished and replaced or at least re-developed; but such uninspiring places still exist in many of our city centres, epitomised in the opening scenes of the BBC TV comedy series 'The Office'. Although filmed in Slough, Berkshire, it could have been in any UK city (and, if you are familiar with the series itself, it could arguably also be about many organisations we see today!). So expression can be negative, as well as positive.

> **'The skyscrapers of New York, Chicago and countless other cities around the world sought to impress and symbolise a successful, dominating organisation.'**

Healthy burgers

Before we focus on physical interior workplace expression – the focus of this chapter – I would like to share a couple of further observations around the concept of expression. First, let's take the fast-food chain *MacDonald's* as an example. Their outlets are instantly recognisable through their (much protected) 'golden arches'

icon – typically displayed on a large, high, exterior structure to attract the attention of passing motorists some distance away (inevitably lit up brightly at night so there is no excuse not to miss it). Nothing subtle here – just basic strong branding. Yes, but in common with many other chain outlets and stores, the consistency of this style of branding, often worldwide, is re-enforcing a more extensive message and that is of the desired promise of utter consistency in terms of products, quality, service and customer experience.

Whether you are a fan of *MacDonalds'* food or of the concept of such standardisation, it has clearly worked for them; not least because of their clever location strategy to optimise the expectation and potential of hungry families, shoppers, travellers or late night revellers. But *MacDonald's* are also very shrewd in terms of their other expression mechanisms – traditionally their TV and billboard promotion, but increasingly through the interior design and imagery within their outlets. The negative connotations associated with burgers and chips and obesity concerns, for example, have been addressed by campaigns to promote their more healthier menu options – with backlit imagery all around of salads, happy people and healthy lifestyles to reassure us that all is well.

Virtual expression

We also need to recognise that all of us are increasingly living and operating in parallel virtual and physical worlds. I remember attending a conference in the early 1990s which has left an impression on me ever since. I have long forgotten the speaker concerned (my apologies to him), but have never forgotten what he said.

> '...for many organisations, their Internet web site is their only "front door".'

His argument was that the power of the Internet would totally change the way organisations promote themselves

and conduct business. As an illustration of such e-commerce (a term yet to be invented at that stage), he boldly stated that most organisations, whether a major high street retailer, a professional body, government organisation or just the local baker or painter and decorator, would no longer need to display its full name, address or telephone number on its bags, cards, shop fronts, paperwork or vans. It would simply need to display its web site address. The conference roared with laughter, seemingly assuming this character to be mad. He was in fact, of course, a very clever futurist.

Now, as we know, the reality is that for many organisations, their Internet web site is their only 'front door'. The design of that site, its ease of use, use of imagery and so on are what portray that organisation's identity to its customers and are the only aspects that are important to its customers.

Examples that come to mind are the likes of easyJet and Ryanair. I have never seen any of their offices. I have no idea what they are like. I hope that they are good places to be and consistent with the pioneering nature of these organisations and their business models and services. But as an online customer, aside from the experience of checking in at airports and flying on the planes, the organisations' front doors are their websites; and I find them very user-friendly and practical (albeit you do learn through experience how to work your way through the websites without incurring potentially undesired extra costs like luggage or insurance!). For other organisations like Amazon, eBay and Google I have no physical relationship at all with them – though am a very regular and satisfied customer.

So expression applies in both the physical and virtual worlds of business; and most organisations will have a need to address both elements to one degree or another. How many times have you looked up the website of a reputable company to be disappointed or frustrated by poor design, illogical navigation or out-of-date content? Indeed, in contrast, the offices or shop windows of these organisations may project a very different and more professional image – but,

increasingly for many organisations, the majority of customers may never have a need or desire to visit these physical sites.

Staff attending job interviews will typically check out the website of their potential employer first, which then may or may not encourage them to pursue employment. Really simple, but important stuff, but so often overlooked. Check out your own organisation's website – see what it tells you!

Inside out

Back to the physical world. So if interior design expression is the new means of making statements and influencing a workforce and/or customers, how does this manifest itself? Once again this is not new. Take a classic example. In my career as a wandering consultant I have spent too much time in hotels, and hotels are a good example of buildings that work hard to communicate a good first impression through their reception spaces. Whether it is to symbolise traditional comfort and service or suggest a more contemporary experience, they do their best to welcome you and entice you to stay.

> **'Staff attending job interviews will typically check out the website of their potential employer first, which then may or may not encourage them to pursue employment.'**

Unfortunately in my experience, typically operating on a corporate budget, the promised glamour ends with the posh carpet as you climb beyond the second floor and my fifth floor bedsit is inevitably a disappointment. So expression also sets expectations, which should ideally be followed through. The superficial use of expression is one we need to watch in the workplace, if it is to be used in a positive way with its occupants.

Another example is that of the top management consultancy firms. Like the original Whitehall Government buildings and, to a larger extent, modern day financial institutions and banks, their internal reception and client-facing hospitality facilities are designed to impress and send out a message of a solid, trusted, well-established and professional organisation. Quality fittings and features are everywhere and no expense is seemingly spared. As a potential client visiting, this may also beg the question of who pays for all this opulence, of course.

Having worked closely with such organisations, there is often a different story once you pass through the client-facing areas into the more general workspace. Typically this is of a different, lower standard, especially for the less senior staff. The comparison is often quite acute, almost disturbing for the escorted visitor. But what does it say to the staff about how the organisation views and values them? As previously stated, expression can work both ways, so needs careful thought and consideration. To be fair, these organisations have slowly recognised this mismatch and now pay as much attention on the positive impact of their 'internal' space.

Changing the scenery

In the workplace context, the internal layout, choice of furnishing, use of colour, imagery and materials, all combine to express a message to its users. This layer of design, below the basic building fabric, is what I call scenery. And, as in the theatrical context, it can be changed relatively easily to update the messaging. Furniture and fittings perhaps not too often (appropriate when a more fundamental refresh is required), but décor, imagery and temporary features more frequently, as required.

Retail outlets, such as shops, employ this change of message and expression frequently in a commercial sense to promote new products and services. Although the space within a *MacDonald's* outlet is the epitome

of efficiency and effectiveness, the style of furnishing and décor is also carefully considered to attract its target customers. Occasionally there is a substantial refit to update and refresh its relevance; but more typically aspects like counter and window graphics are changed on a daily basis to promote the latest food products and prices (and more subtly its image as implied earlier).

Environmental awareness is another growing area where organisations are very quick to use strong expression messaging to associate itself positively with these topical areas of corporate responsibility. The walls of *Marks and Spencer's* food halls are currently adorned in graphics promoting its sustainable approach to sourcing and producing the food it sells. This seemingly sells better than promoting taste or value at present. Well-lit food presentation and further imagery ensure you cannot resist buying.

> 'In the workplace... the internal layout, choice of furnishing, use of colour, imagery and materials, all combine to express a message to its users.'

Just look around you. Whether you are shopping, eating or buying a car, interior expression is everywhere – sending messages to influence, inspire and attract.

Go for it

So with all this in mind, why are so many workplaces today still so bland, resorting to the safe common denominator of grey or beige corporate interior dullness? In these days of trying to manage change, attract and retain talented people, encourage creativity and innovation and improve business focus, this just doesn't make sense any more. This is not really about cost or fashion, just good business sense – which in other areas of commerce, such as retail, organisations have always been so quick to grasp and exploit.

So the time has come to look at interior design and associated features in a new light, as a key communication device, not just to customers and visitors but also to the staff themselves, the major workplace occupants.

I don't believe any organisation sets out to produce or sell bland products and services, or whose values are about being restrained, boring and anonymous, yet that is the message that many organisations seem to want to express, particularly to their own staff. To properly support organisational business and cultural objectives, in increasingly competitive times, there is a need now, more than ever, to positively connect and focus staff on desired business direction, standards and outputs through a suitably effective *and* expressive workplace.

> '...why are so many workplaces today still so bland, resorting to the safe common denominator of grey or beige corporate interior dullness?'

Landscape painting

Décor provides the backdrop for interior design. On the whole, it doesn't really cost any more to create attractive décor than it does a bland decor. Creativity, imagination and perhaps some courage are the key additional requirements, not materials or labour. Professional interior design advice is always recommended in any case.

Nowadays, of course, everyone is an expert in internal design, informed by a myriad of property development and interior design make-over TV programmes and magazines. All the more reason now for consulting with the workforce in a controlled and more manageable way, otherwise you may get hundreds of conflicting opinions to deal with. Most staff appreciate the opportunity to make small choices within a fixed framework, but are happy that the bigger decisions

(overall furniture or colour schemes) are made by the professionals and are respectful of this form of leadership.

Using a timeless, contemporary look with subtle splashes of colour can also help ensure the décor does not outdate too quickly, and even if you choose to use the latest trend in bold or pastel colours, it is very easy to re-paint a wall if the colour becomes less trendy over time. Colour can often be added through furniture like soft seating, and such features work best against a plainer wall and carpet backdrop. Colour can also be used to support 'way finding' within a large or complex building – identifying different sections or zones. Colour and other symbolism (even artistic wording) might also be used to symbolise the use and function of space, for example quiet areas, shared areas, interactive spaces and so on.

> **'Nowadays, of course, everyone is an expert in internal design, informed by a myriad of property development and interior design make-over TV programmes and magazines.'**

Clever use of colour can also, through illusion, help make narrow spaces wider or low areas higher. Use of low-key colours for repetitive items like desks and task chairs can also help avoid exaggerating these features and emphasising the undesired impression of a 'max-packed' office and its rows and rows of desks.

Use of sustainable materials in furniture, carpeting and workplace features, or having displays that monitor and highlight the 'green' credentials of a building and its operation, will add further positive and appealing messages about corporate responsibility to its occupants.

A trick that painters and landscape gardeners have often used to increase the visual appeal of their creations is to avoid a scenario where everything is immediately obvious and visible. By presenting more than one route through

> 'The workplace... will need to compete with a range of other physical and virtual work opportunities. It will need to attract its users in new ways and reinforce its value in ways it has never needed to do before.'

the scene they have created and applying different perspectives and textures, they encourage the eye to linger and explore, creating a sense of depth, intrigue and interest. On the contrary, there's nothing worse than walking into an open workspace and instantly seeing a vast prairie of regimented grey desks and filing cabinets.

More creative layout, use of colour and graphics, ceiling and lighting features, variations in floor coverings, screening features and so on will all help create a workplace that is more satisfying to see and work in. Furthermore, this will create a place that says something positive to its visitors and occupants. As my mother would often tell me – 'you only get one chance to make a first impression'. The immediate impact of design and expression, in this context, will have a lasting effect and influence on attitudes, morale and motivation of the workforce.

Details count

I once implemented an interesting, early pioneering workplace pilot in the early 1990s. Despite investing heavily in state-of-the-art (at that time) furniture and technology, it was actually the little design details, which at the time I took some risks over, which attracted most of the positive feedback. And these details clearly motivated staff to commit to the brave new work practice changes being asked of them. These details included the bold wall colours, lighting features, sofas and cushions, a projected clock, artwork and graphics and even a fish tank. My adherence to feng shui principles, by accident rather than design, also seemed to go down well. I really learnt about the power of design on that project and how details really do count – experience that has stood me well in the years that have followed.

In the chapters that follow, the importance of workplace expression will be explored to an even more significant level. The workplace, as we are learning, will need to re-invent and re-establish a new role in the context of our increasingly diverse workstyles and work options. It will need to compete with a range of other physical and virtual work opportunities. It will need to attract its users in new ways and reinforce its value in ways it has never needed to do before. Such is the power of expression. Such is the new workplace challenge.

E-work

The office workplace exists to support the function of office work. Pretty obvious, I guess. As discussed in earlier chapters, the nature of the office workplace has evolved over time to reflect the changing nature of work, albeit perhaps not quite as appropriately or responsively as it might have, but work and the nature of the workforce is continuing to rapidly change and evolve, almost unrecognisably. The impact this will have on the definition of what a workplace is, will demand new thinking. This chapter explores the most significant drivers impacting how we should respond in developing our workplace. So, if you have well-established guidelines or policies driving your workplace strategy, now is perhaps the time to throw them away.

5 E-work

Work – but not as we know it

The office workplace exists to support the function of office work. Pretty obvious, I guess. As discussed in earlier chapters, the nature of the office workplace has evolved over time to reflect the changing nature of work, albeit perhaps not quite as appropriately or responsively as it might have, but work and the nature of the workforce is continuing to rapidly change and evolve, almost unrecognisably. The impact this will have on the definition of what a workplace is, will demand new thinking. This chapter explores the most significant drivers impacting how we should respond in developing our workplace. So, if you have well-established guidelines or policies driving your workplace strategy, now is perhaps the time to throw them away.

We have reached a new phase of change in the concept of work, driven by technology-enabled opportunities and changing economic drivers unimaginable even a few years ago, as well as by associated shifts in our attitudes and expectations. The potential for the workplace to fall adrift from the work it is supporting is significant; so a new understanding of what *work* means is required if we are to provide the right sort of work-*'places'* in the future. This means challenging all conventional thinking around the work and workplace relationship and being prepared to consider, or more accurately, invent new models and solutions.

Work and technology relationship

One thing is clear: work has become increasingly enabled by, and dependent upon, technology, which has been the main influence on its development in recent years. The two are intrinsically linked. And whilst technology is offering ever-increasing new opportunities and options for work – e-work if you like – it is also requiring new understanding and disciplines if it is to be most appropriately *optimised*.

Perhaps the biggest impact in recent times is in the ability technology has provided to allow work to take place across different locations, both within the office and, significantly, beyond the office shell. The monopoly that the traditional office workplace had once with facilitating work has now been broken and technology has almost taken its place. But how has this happened – and what will it mean for us in the future? Also how can we best harness the power and potential of technology to our advantage?

> **'The potential for the workplace to fall adrift from the work it is supporting is significant...'**

Who's driving who?

No aspect of office work or commerce is untouched, it seems, by technology and, more recently, the power of the Internet. Information, knowledge and communication, the lifeblood of business, lies entirely in its hands – sometimes controlled by us, often seemingly out of our control. Appropriately harnessing technology is, and has always been, the key challenge.

Looking back we can see how technology has taken on much of the mundane, process aspects of office-work, allowing office workers to be freed up to add value in other ways and evolve their roles. The focus has moved to the intelligent filtering, interpretation and application of data and associated development of working relationships, collaboration and team-work – giving rise to a new breed of knowledge-workers and networkers. To further support this autonomy and empowerment, technology also moved from centralised control and processing to personal desktop computing.

However, this also had the counter-effect of information and knowledge not being shared in some quarters, of duplicated data and effort, and increasing 'silo-working'. Knowledge was power and often misused in the interest of individuals, not the organisation. The explosion of the Internet added to the

mix in offering seemingly infinite and unmanageable access to information choices. There was an information overload and initially no corporate approach to managing this phenomenon.

Some recent statistics[1] that I recently read suggest that up to 30 per cent of the Internet, at any time, is new – such is the generation rate of information. The even scarier statistic is that 161 exabytes (that is 161 billion gigabytes, to you and me!) of digital information existed in 2006 – 3 million times more information than provided by all the books ever written. Goodness knows who does all the counting and what the current figure might be, but no wonder our brains ache sometimes! I used to think that my children had it easier at school, having access to the knowledge and information of the Internet; but they face the same challenge as we do in filtering and managing the staggering wraths of information that is out there.

> **'Knowledge was power and often misused in the interest of individuals, not the organisation.'**

However, intranets, document management systems and, most recently, thin client technologies have all supported a reversal trend to use technology in a more controlled, structured and secure manner within organisations to better manage and optimise its role in supporting work and business.

Technology also increased the speed of work. I remember working in the Civil Service, in the pre-e-mail early-1980s, sending off paper memos to seek inputs or decisions, not expecting a paper or verbal (via a scheduled meeting) response for at least a week. Nowadays, we expect e-mail responses within a day or even hour (for those with BlackBerry or similar devices) and we are

---

1   Source: Flip by Peter Sheadon 2007/*Time* magazine/IDC.

disappointed if we don't get text responses within a few minutes. Such is the pace of communication now and work output expectations.

This of course puts unending pressure on us as workers to be always available and contactable and to deliver outputs in increasingly impossible timelines. Management have seized on these opportunities to demand more and more of us. Technology as an enabler and as a liberator also can become our master and captor.

Pointed heads

Without wishing to offend anyone, much of my work experience has revealed that those involved in the development and delivery of technology solutions in the workplace are a rather unique breed of person. One colleague of mine affectionately referred to them as 'pointed-headed' people. Not very fair, of course, but this is perhaps a reflection of the mutual lack of understanding and frustration that has existed around the work, workplace and technology relationship.

> 'Nowadays, we expect e-mail responses within a day or even hour... and we are disappointed if we don't get text responses within a few minutes.'

From the technical point of view, the exciting power and possibilities of technology, which is the passion of these specialists, has had to be countered with the need for reliability and business continuity and security. Such risk measures have inevitably served to constrain and control the application of technology in the workplace. This enables an important safe level of service and support to be provided, but this also leads to perceptions of inflexibility and lack of response to ever-changing business needs. This mutual frustration is often heightened by the fact that whilst we, as users, increasingly are asking

for more, we also consistently fail to make full or proper use of the technology we have.

This is aggravated further by our often being given over complicated technology beyond our requirements – telephones with functions we will never use, software that is over-integrated with other applications and, in the home context, TV remote controls with around 30 buttons too many!

The truth is that our demands are often selective, based on our new experiences as consumers, embracing niche technology in our homes and everyday lives to match our transforming lifestyles. If we can turn our front rooms into a home cinema and interactive games centre (with the help of our children, naturally), why can't the office even come close to being so responsive? However, corporate technology, if I can call it that, by its very nature of scale and dependence has to come in more standardised and established packages and will inevitably be perceived as slower to evolve.

> '...whilst we, as users, increasingly are asking for more, we also consistently fail to make full or proper use of the technology we have.'

Our expectations have also changed significantly over the years. At one time, as simple office technology-users, we took what we were given, often reluctantly, and did not have the knowledge to question or challenge. We were in awe of what technology could do and accepted, as normal, many of its idiosyncrasies. Technology beyond the workplace was much more limited and so we had nothing to make comparisons with. The power and control was with the technology departments, not the workforce. Now that scenario is partly in reverse. I say partly, because whilst we have abundant choice and options now, the need for understanding, disciplines and skills in our use of technology and the related workstyles that we chose is now more important than ever.

Mobile telephony and computing

A really significant part of business (and leisure) technology developments
has been the mobile phone. It is hard to conceive a time when we didn't
have such devices and how we existed without their convenience. I can still
remember the earliest mobile phones. As
with early laptops, they were big, ugly
and expensive – and by today's standards,
provided miniscule capabilities – but how
that has now changed. The UK is one of a
number of countries now which has more
mobile phones than people[2] and such
phone functionality is becoming ever-more
sophisticated beyond basic voice and (the probably more important) text
communications – with e-mail, Internet browsing, cameras and GPS[3] features
becoming standard.

> **'The power and control
> was with the technology
> departments, not the
> workforce.'**

I must admit I am not a fan of over-convergence of such devices,
primarily because their scale makes them unworkable. Indeed, as an aside,
I am amazed at how a generation of cash-rich, but visually challenged (in
terms of using small font-displays and key pads) older consumers are being
potentially ignored in this market. Not that I see myself as old or cash-rich
just yet! I suggest that the development of more accessible, less youth-
orientated products could become the next big growth area for this saturated
industry.

In addition to portable phones, there is also an array of portable hand-held
devices with PC capabilities – such as the Blackberry or i-phone – typically
combined with a phone, which add to the choices and flexibility. These devices,
as an alternative or compliment to laptops, are helping to enable an increasing

---

2   CIA statistics – www.cia.gov/library/publications/the-world-factbook.

3   Global Positioning Software, often referred to as satellite navigation.

portion of the workforce to work, even if on an occasional basis, from any location, which may include home.

The advent of office-based cordless or DECT[4] phones has had more of a significant development for work within the office – helping the introduction of open-plan environments and wider ranges of new

> **'The real liberator for laptop users is the advent of wireless connectivity...'**

worksettings by enabling staff to move away from their desk or move to another setting to take or make a call to aid confidentiality, as well as reduce disturbance for others.

Cordless office telephony has not been universally adopted, however, and interestingly many office workers use a combination of desktop phone and personal or work mobile phone to deal with the dynamics of the office. The ability to easily transfer a 'virtual' phone extension from one position to another is another option here, made easier with more recent VOIP[5] developments. Most recently, the advent of 'dual-mode' phones (that act as internal network phones in the office and convert to public networks out of the office) may provide a simpler solution to the more nomadic workers.

Mobile telephony clearly provides one level of liberation for the office worker (within and beyond the office). Of course, the laptop computer has also supported this flexibility – becoming more portable, more powerful and more affordable over time. Laptops are often allocated, however, on the basis of status, rather than functional need; and thus many laptops never leave their office desks. But even for the more dynamic workers, network connectivity in the office is often cumbersome beyond the desk and 'docking stations' designed to enable full workstation set-up, often restrict the use of

---

4   DECT – Digital Enhanced Cordless Telecommunications.

5   Voice Over Internet Protocol – integration of voice and data communications through phones and PCs.

incompatible laptops between desks. The increasing ability to log on (with a 'roaming profile') to any workstation gets around this to some extent, using others' or shared PCs.

The real liberator for laptop users is the advent of wireless connectivity – within the office (for internal networked applications) and also outside the office via the Internet. There are still many security concerns around this, especially in the Government sector; but to truly optimise the advocated landscaped office and its rich mix of worksettings, the empowerment provided by wireless computing (along with telephony) is almost essential. These developments are unfolding in parallel to developments in working practices that see increasing abilities (and 'permissions') to work outside the office at other locations, placing a wider context to these office challenges.

The ultimate flexibility will come, of course, with wireless power – and this is already a reality in the shape of a concept being tested known as WiTricity, based on non-radioactive electromagnetic fields. Another development, by Microsoft known as 'Surface', sees the integration of (multi-user) technology touch screens into furniture, such as table tops and counters. Although initially envisaged as supporting customer interfaces in shops, hotels and restaurants, this could easily be adopted as a further 'work-anywhere-collaboratively' tool for the dynamic office. Indeed, conceivably, this technology will become the basis of the future desk for all of us and certainly the office reception or service counter.

There is, of course, a limitation here in terms of the dependency on a specialist piece of potentially expensive hardware (in whatever form it takes), although costs will inevitably drop to support mainstream adoption over time. Much better, however, would be an ability to transform any surface, wherever we happen to be, to support such interactive functionality, triggered by discrete portable technologies we can carry about with us (perhaps even 'wear' as part of our clothing) and simple hand/finger movements. This is something currently

being explored by top technology experts, including Indian guru Pranav Mistry,[6] who through his SixthSense inventions aims to enable new interactions between everyday physical objects and the power of the virtual world. Examples here would be normal newspapers that can be turned into speech or video or the ability to take photos through a virtual camera gestured by our hands.

The Internet

> 'The ultimate flexibility will come, of course, with wireless power...'

The other extremely significant element of technology development in recent times is, of course, the Internet or World Wide Web, as it was originally named. It has grown, in relatively recent years, from an almost geek-run science and military-orientated joining-up of networks initiative (inter-networking, using common protocols) in the 1960s into the global phenomenon we know today.

It has transformed the way we manage, share and access information and knowledge – impacting, over time, all aspects of our lives. In particular in the way we educate and learn, as well as undertake business and commerce – breaking through time and geography boundaries in our increasingly 24/7 existences. It has even, most significantly, impacted our leisure time and the way we socialise and network on a personal level.

The initial rush to commercialise and invest in new Internet-enabled markets saw the rise and fall of the dot.com boom in the 1990s. But recovery from this has seen the Internet continue to grow in use and sophistication in a more stable manner, supported by ever-improving networking and bandwidth capabilities and growing public confidence, knowledge and skills, particularly

---

6   www.pranavmistry.com

beyond the office in the public and domestic domains. The Internet truly impacts so much of our daily lives and routines now, it is hard to imagine life without it. Indeed try to convince someone in their early teens that the Internet is such a relatively recent 'invention' and they simply just won't believe you (or they will look at you like you were 100 years old!)

I referred to Internet socialising and it is worth mentioning the exponential growth of online social networking that has occurred within the last decade. I am thinking of the likes of Facebook, Flickr, MySpace, YouTube and Twitter. Most teenagers today will be very familiar with these sites and would be expert contributors to them – publishing online content and establishing relationships in ways the office environment would be proud of. Interestingly, Twitter seems to have become adopted as the media favoured for adults and business (and entertainment) professionals – albeit the diary-style content often seems incredibly 'teenage-like' to me!!

For years we have struggled to encourage office use of electronic document management and intranets and blogs, with fairly slow initial uptake. But as new generations of workers arrive at the workplace they will expect to do the majority of their knowledge-exchange, discussions and networking online; and will value face-to-face encounters, as a less frequent occurrence, in a different way. The organisations currently barring staff access to such networking sites or indeed the Internet as a whole are, in this context, being very short-sighted. Such Dickensian attitudes will simply make a generation of new workers walk.

> '...try to convince someone in their early teens that the Internet is such a relatively recent "invention" and they simply just won't believe you (or they will look at you like you were 100 years old!)'

Having said this, my earlier comment about the frivolous nature of certain *twitter* use does suggest that this is an area that still needs to be well managed by organisations, so that precious work-time is not lost by an over-zealous and misguided desire by all to socialise and keep in touch. Like the wider information explosion of the Internet, the challenge for us all is to skilfully filter, manage and optimise the value of such electronic information sources.

Work and place relationship

Probably most significantly of all, is the impact that technology has had over the 'place' of work. Originally technology linked places rather than people – with connections made always through fixed physical elements like the office telephone or desktop PC, which in turn was fixed to furniture, that is, the desk. This reinforced the need and value of coming to the office and the role of the office desk. Now such outmoded 'middle-men' are no longer required, as we connect directly to each other through small portable devices. Ultimately, it is inevitable that even these may disappear to be replaced by technology that is embedded into our clothes (or even implanted into our skin!)

> '...organisations currently barring staff access to... networking sites or... the Internet as a whole are... being very short-sighted. Such Dickensian attitudes will simply make a generation of new workers walk.'

Private or public wireless broadband is contributing further to the ability for people to work together remotely and in real time – breaking physical, geographical and temporal boundaries. Two or more people can visually connect through web-cam PC-based video conferencing and actively share and edit documents across locations. Work has infinite choice and possibilities now. Work is everywhere and anywhere you want it to be. Work is what you do, not

somewhere you go. Work is now e-work. And if you can work anywhere, why would you come to the office, particularly if it involved a tortuous commute? Especially in these environmentally-conscious times.

The office workplace is no longer the only, or most appropriate, container for the process of work – individual, concentrated work tasks in particular – so all those involved in the management, development and supply of office workspace need to re-focus on new requirements, opportunities and solutions, as the traditional solutions may soon be a thing of the past. A wake-up call, for sure.

> '...if you can work anywhere, why would you come to the office, particularly if it involved a tortuous commute?'

These changes are allowing traditionally mobile staff to stay connected and avoid unnecessary trips to the office but, more significantly, are allowing previously office-based staff the choice to work at other locations, like home, if this supports personal and business needs. Typically not as home-based workers but as occasional home-workers – an important distinction in terms of employee terms and conditions. Even traditional office-bound roles like secretaries can be liberated. If the boss is not in the office, they don't need to be either to provide the support and services that are required!

This is presenting opportunities for better work-life balance, reduced travelling and increased motivation and morale, as well as positive environmental and local community/economy impacts. But the discipline of retaining an occasional presence in the office has become essential to retain social and knowledge links to colleagues, and even more so for the organisation to retain its values, culture and identity.

Big brother

One interesting area of technology development is around location-based media, linked to GPS capabilities, which effectively allow devices (such as phones or laptops) to be geographically tracked and traced. With a distributed workforce, the benefits of being able to understand where people are beyond the office and find them within the office are clear. Obviously there is a line where this may infringe privacy, but such facilities can be disabled by the user. Another application of this technology would allow users to approach worksettings, be recognised automatically by the technology there, and then be given a personalised set-up, based on a registered profile.

In a similar way to the manner in which *Google* presents online adverts to us based on our inputs (and thus interest), such location-based technologies can also be used to provide the most relevant location-based services to workers, within or beyond the office – for example, details of hotels nearest the location you happen to be working on that day.

> **'Managers need to learn how to measure performance by outputs and outcomes and not inputs (that is, time at the desk)...'**

Presence

In a similar manner, the ability to identify who else is online at any moment in time can help optimise and focus web communication and 'e-working'. Web-based conferencing, e-mailing and document-sharing in 'real time', supported by products like *Microsoft's 'Office Communicator'*, fully exploit this concept of online presence. Such an additional perspective around virtual collaboration is particularly useful in emergency scenarios, when you can't simply leave to chance that someone will be out there and able to respond.

The flip-side to this, of course, is that in the office scenario we may no longer be able to simply assume in future that somebody is 'present' in the office and available at our beck and call. As in the virtual world, such interactions need to be appropriately planned and tracked through responsible diary management and basic communication protocols!

Homework

The development of home-working policies has been an important, if slow, part of the overall distributed working development. Now various models exist – formal and informal. Most home-working is typically done on an ad-hoc, occasional basis (perhaps once a week, sometimes more) to meet certain business or personal needs. In these circumstances, the workers main place of employment is the office. Those that are more permanently based at home are usually referred to as teleworkers – and often these people have office-based processing jobs that have simply been re-located to the home.

Policies around health and safety (often self-assessment), associated expenses (often paid as a flat allowance) and data security are now well developed in many organisations to support more typical home-working policies; and often it is the culture, and the 'presenteesim' factor previously referred to, that gets in the way of real progress.

Managers need to learn how to measure performance by outputs and outcomes and not inputs (that is, time at the desk) and they also need to learn how to manage teams they don't see everyday. Guidance and training for managers is a critical aspect of introducing home-working, so often overlooked.

It is a manager who has to consider and decide, fairly, whether a request to work from home can be granted. It is a manager who has to ensure that business productivity or individual's well-being does not suffer as a result of

such working. It is the manager who will give confidence to the home-worker in adopting this workstyle in a professional and sensible way. However, don't forget to incorporate desk-sharing considerations (as covered in Chapter 2) as part of these developments. This will be less popular but will serve to highlight those who are serious about taking up regular and properly supported homeworking.

There are certainly lessons to be learnt here for any organisations embarking on this for the first time. I do recall one organisation, based in the semi-rural North-East of England, that spent a number of years developing a very commendable home-working policy, which many other organisations subsequently used as an exemplar. The problem was, however, that there was no real take-up of this work option by its own workforce. It all seemed like a waste of effort and some of the objectives of the initiative, in terms of freeing up office space, were unable to be realised.

What was overlooked was the nature of the workforce and their 'appetite' for such change. Comprising of mainly locally-based working mums, these staff looked forward to coming to work for the social benefits, as much as anything else. Why on earth would they want to spend all day alone at home while the rest of their families were away at work or school? No-one bothered to ask if they were interested.

On the flip-side of this is the experience of another organisation which I supported in introducing flexible working, including home-working, which they were keen to promote. Here a comprehensive questionnaire was issued to staff to ascertain levels of interest and potential – and the feedback was

staggering for management. Over 80 per cent of staff revealed that they already worked from home, albeit on an informal basis; with half of that number stating that they worked from home in addition to their day in the office, that is, in evenings and at weekends.

Far from hoping to ascertain levels of interest, these results sounded real alarm bells in that home-working was being undertaken without proper structure, guidance or support, potentially to the detriment rather than the benefit of staff work-life balance. I suspect a lot more informal home-working goes on than many organisations are really aware of or have taken the time to understand and assess. Definitely one to watch, as this is such a popular work option these days.

Third place world

Home isn't the only alternative workplace – a range of 'third' place options are available – private, public and semi-public – such as client or customer offices, local or regional centres, on-demand serviced offices, hotels, cafes and, with wireless connectivity, indeed most areas of the city or rural landscape. The differentiation between public, semi-public (or privileged) and private space is significant in terms of access, security, facilities and costs.

For example, e-mail-related work is something, armed with access to wireless broadband, which can be done almost anywhere and in most public spaces. However, more specific tasks, like printing or holding a formal meeting, might require the use of local or regional shared work centres or on-demand facility, which typically involves a fee or membership – hence the semi-public, privileged description. Access to secure, internal databases or indeed a group

> 'The differentiation between public, semi-public (or privileged) and private space is significant in terms of access, security, facilities and costs.'

of work colleagues may only be available in the privacy and convenience of an organisation's own office building or a secure networked alternative location, like a regional office.

The distributed workplace

Given these parameters, it is easy to see how the various choices and options of potential work 'places' that are available to workers (assuming an organisation's culture and policies permit), also have their respective relevancies. At a strategic level, you can also see how an organisation might chose to utilise all these possibilities to reduce its owned office space and associated costs – supplementing it with a mix of on-demand, pay-as-you-go arrangements as well as more public no-cost facilities.

For example, an organisation might choose to only own its 'private workspaces' which might include a smaller headquarters for corporate functions in a city centre, plus some specialist buildings for, say, IT and training facilities in a more out-of-town location. All other workspace, perhaps their local offices or out-sourced functions, would be provided by other organisations on a flexible 'pay as you use' basis. Additionally, much of their client-facing workforce, armed with appropriate technologies, would use a range of client and public spaces, at no cost, to carry out the majority of their work activities.

Within the above scenario are elements of 'public', 'privileged' and 'private' workspaces – which may be found at different sites, or in the case of the headquarters building, may exist together in one site, – with appropriate subtle security accesses in place (for example, a public atrium, shared organisational support areas and private team spaces).

An entire organisational strategy might be re-written to take these new options into account and achieve significant savings and flexibility around

planned, and importantly unknown, future business operations. See Figure 5.1.

You can also see how, when an organisation wants to speculatively set itself up in a new location, even country, the traditional cost, hassle and risk of setting up a new temporary office location can be eliminated, at least until the business is more established. Such 'presence' and operation in this new location can be provided very easily and adequately initially from a hotel room or apartment, accompanied by a suitably locally-tailored website.

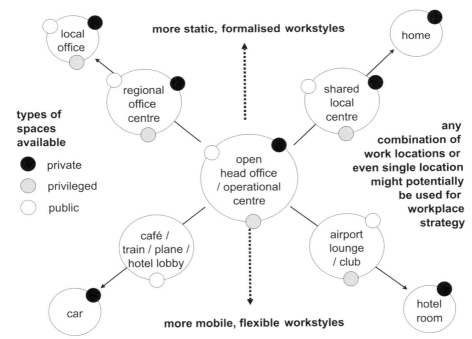

Figure 5.1   The hub and spoke workplace model
Source: DEGW/Bell.

Another variation here is that of organisations sharing the same workspace, where there are no commercial, customer or time conflicts and, as can often occur, there are mutual benefits in doing so. There are already high street examples such as Abbey (part of the Santander group), Carphone Warehouse and Costa Coffee coming together in the same premises – each one attracting potential customers for each other and the economies of scale enabling a much larger and more attractive 'place' for people to come to and, importantly, linger.

The partnerships between Tesco and Texaco providing complimentary retail services from the same petrol forecourt location is another example. There is a Shell training centre in the Netherlands that turns into a Holiday Inn at weekends – both using similar facilities but with different customers and different patterns of demand in terms of time. No doubt there will be more and more such alliances. It is simple business common sense.

The distributed workplace model

International workplace consultants, DEGW, have developed a distributed workplace model (Figure 5.2) that maps out an even broader picture of the potential locations of work. It recognises the three distinctions of private, privilege and public physical workspaces, but also highlights their virtual equivalents – in terms of the public access of the Internet, the semi-private technology of extranets and the private technology associated with organisational intranets and secure systems.

I guess the ultimate virtual world is where the all physical elements are also virtual and simulated, as experienced through sophisticated 'games', such as *Second Life*.[7] These worlds convey a sense of presence lacking in other forms

---

7   *Second Life* – user defined virtual world, where real life, including commerce, is simulated – where avatars (virtual representations of people) interact.

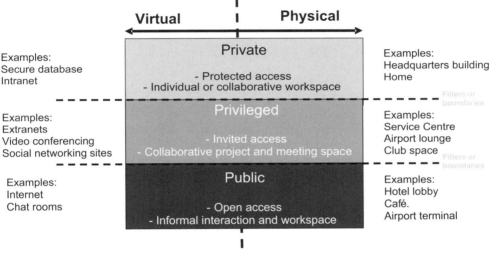

Virtual		Physical

Examples:
Secure database
Intranet

Private

- Protected access
- Individual or collaborative workspace

Examples:
Headquarters building
Home

Filters or boundaries

Examples:
Extranets
Video conferencing
Social networking sites

Privileged

- Invited access
- Collaborative project and meeting space

Examples:
Service Centre
Airport lounge
Club space

Filters or boundaries

Examples:
Internet
Chat rooms

Public

- Open access
- Informal interaction and workspace

Examples:
Hotel lobby
Café.
Airport terminal

Figure 5.2   The distributed working model
Source: DEGW.

of digital media, making them extremely realistic. As such, real relationships and commercial trading are already happening in these parallel existences; and the application of such technology in the context of future work may too be a reality in future.

Video-collaboration

Closer to today's reality, however, is video-conferencing, perhaps the most obvious bridge between the physical and virtual world. It is a fairly well-established communications method nowadays, although early applications of this technology were not very successful, mainly because they were an extremely poor substitute for physical interaction, where facial expressions and eye contact are so important.

> '...the concept of technology-enabled multi-locational working is now much more natural to us than ever before, especially for younger workers.'

Today's video-conferencing, whether at laptop to laptop level (web-cams) or more significantly in specialist room facilities, is much more life-like and effective, thanks to screen, camera and data bandwidth improvements. Full multi-screen walls in specialist rooms allow groups to interact with each other from different locations, at actual size-dimensions, almost as if they are sitting formally at the other side of the table; with the camera(s) deliberately positioned to facilitate effective virtual eye contact.

A new portable *Microsoft* table-top device, *'round table'*, uses 360-degree cameras and panoramic display to enable such inter-group virtual interaction to take place in less sophisticated, informal settings.

Interestingly, the growth of such virtual-world supporting technologies within the office requires space that is normally unattractive for most other office activities – that is, areas where natural light is poorer – and therefore does not compete for the same resources and characteristics, offering increased opportunities to optimise all areas of physical office space.

There is no doubt that virtual-physical bridges such as video-conferencing will grow, adding further to the 'workscape' of work 'place' options and opportunities. Video-cams on mobile phones, for example, will become much more commonplace and provide ultimate portability and informality for such interactions.

Distributed workers

The parallel development of mindsets to exploit this new framework for work is, of course, important. As we have learnt before, simply providing solutions

does not necessarily mean they will be taken up and used. However, the work arena is now much more aligned to our everyday lives and the concept of technology-enabled multi-locational working is now much more natural to us than ever before, especially for younger workers. Equally, organisations have learnt to apply effort to the necessary cultural changes required to mobilise and embed new ways of working. Figure 5.3 tracks the attitudinal changes or 'journey' for individuals as they get further involved in distributed working.

Of course, career models are also changing. There's no such thing as a job for life anymore we are told and, increasingly, people are more frequently moving employers, even careers, or are having more than one professional job – portfolio working, as I call it. Increasingly, many are self-employed but there are growing numbers of employee-status entrepreneurs who 'sell their talent' project-working across different parts of an organisation or even across a number of organisations. I count myself among this number nowadays.

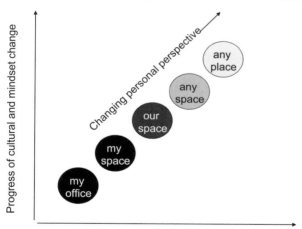

Figure 5.3   Relationship between individual attitudinal change and distributed working

Source: Bell.

The office niche

In many respects, the last few pages and Figure 5.1 outline the full arena of potential workplaces and the context in which the physical office workplace we know and love has to exist.

However, given all these competing virtual and physical options and opportunities – exactly where does the physical workplace fit? Where is its place? What will make it a rewarding and worthwhile destination of choice? What does it need to provide in terms of facilities or experiences to define its role and distinction and differentiate it? How far does it need to change from its existing state?

> **'Organisations... will need to make sure the office workplace can become a destination of choice for workers...'**

Well I hope most of the answers have been covered to a large extent, through this book, although perhaps the final 'experience' chapter is the most powerful of all in this context. The 'experience' emotion can be the most compelling of all triggers in attracting 'hearts and minds'.

Work, especially the more individual, concentrative tasks, can be done in a number of places – but the office workplace should be one of them. Not everyone is able to or wishes to work from home. Not everyone has a workstyle that allows them frequent access to alternative places, like cafes.

More collaborative, interactive, perhaps project-based work can also be done in a number of places, but may need access to certain equipment or facilities or, more importantly, people. Again the office workplace should be one of these places and arguably the best place for these activities, assuming it can meet the needs and expectations of workers in this respect.

Organisations for their part will need to make sure the office workplace can become a destination of choice for workers, if they are to retain the important concepts of corporate culture, values, identity, sense of belonging and centre of knowledge for its workforce – and all the benefits these can bring.

This may mean a smaller office. This may mean a different distribution of, or location for, the office. This may mean shared premises with other organisations and this will certainly mean a very different look and feel for the office, in terms of its design, facilities and services. But the office workplace position and role is assured, I believe, as long as organisations can respond to the changes now required.

All in all, this suggests a strategy that makes no assumptions about the continuation of a retained, traditional role for the office workplace, but rather focuses on establishing a new case for a compelling, niche facility that can underpin the very existence and stability of the modern organisation in a mad, fast-changing, confusing world!

Experience

I started this book, through its preface, in a remote but beautiful part of Thailand; part of a holiday that was to enable a level of reflection, inspiration, relaxation, excitement and companionship that my day-to-day existence struggles to provide a window for. For this reason, I value my holidays for the experience, albeit short term, that they bring. I try to get away whenever I can, not necessarily lavish holidays, but just the odd weekend somewhere different.

6 Experience

The value of experience

I started this book, through its preface, in a remote but beautiful part of Thailand; part of a holiday that was to enable a level of reflection, inspiration, relaxation, excitement and companionship that my day-to-day existence struggles to provide a window for. For this reason, I value my holidays for the experience, albeit short term, that they bring. I try to get away whenever I can, not necessarily lavish holidays, but just the odd weekend somewhere different.

I wasn't always like this though. I do recall, some time back, viewing holidays purely as an extravagant expense. Yes, there were two weeks of fun, quality family-time and a degree of escapism – but in my eyes the money spent could have alternatively provided months of food and petrol, enabled those DIY projects to be completed and even help towards that desperately needed replacement car. I even recall, shame to say it, choosing to spend a good portion of that expensive holiday-time actually working anyway – completing pieces of work and preparing for the next project – keen to keep on top of things and make all the right career impressions.

> 'In a time when most *products* are capable of meeting our basic needs or specifications, experience is the one thing that can differentiate one from another and influence our choice.'

Looking back over the years I can barely now remember what some of those areas of work were and what real relevance or difference, in hindsight, they made to my career or indeed my life or the wider world around me. It's all a bit of a blur, all a bit meaningless. However, my memories of holidays over the years – key moments in any case – are very clear; and indeed these are the experiences I choose to recall in conversation or private thoughts, time and time again. These are the experiences that have really marked the progress, learning and influences through my life and that are truly valued.

Making a difference

On a similar vein, I am not a fan of fairground rides and am certainly not into extreme sports (although in a rare moment of madness I once white-water-rafted down the Zambezi and was seconds away from bungee-jumping from a bridge in the same locale, before bottling out!) but I can understand the draw and buzz of such memorable experiences. Indeed, extreme sports are an indication of the need to increasingly take that one step further to create an experience that can be differentiated from our more everyday events and encounters, sporting or otherwise, which increasingly cease to satisfy us. This is a growing trend as different products, services and facilities compete for our previous time and attention, amidst the seemingly endless choices now available.

It is a direct (or indirect, if recommended) positive and rewarding experience that influences our choice of restaurants, hotels, pubs, clubs, shopping, homes, holidays and even our jobs. Experiences also influence our choice of car, clothes or household appliances – or perhaps more accurately, the advertising for these products suggest an experience to us that is attractive – promising to make us feel better, make life easier or make us the envy of our friends. In a time when most *products* are capable of meeting our basic needs or specifications, experience is the one thing that can differentiate one from another and influence our choice. And we remember bad experiences as well as, if not better than, good experiences, so getting the experience right is critical. Advertisers realise this and so must, in time, employers. The workplace and associated working practices and culture play a significant part of this increasingly important new 'work experience' or proposition.

Whilst references to holidays and bungee jumping might appear a bit of a diversion from the subject of this book, it is a suitable introduction to the concept of 'experience'. Indeed you can probably see where this may be leading in terms of the office workplace and the daily experience it can bring to its users and visitors. But before I get into that, I would just like to explore briefly

a couple more everyday-life commercial examples that further demonstrate the power of experience and the need to recognise and harness it – lessons that the workplace needs to heed.

Movie-magic

Firstly, the resilience of the cinema. Although perhaps never to return to its heyday of the 1930s and despite the demolition or conversion of most original buildings now into modern shopping malls or super-pubs and clubs (another experienced-based phenomenon), a new style of super-cinema has emerged in recent times. Now offering wider movie choices, the very latest releases, lounge-style seating, huge screens and surround sound, the new cinemas promise much. They are also often located in out-of-town retail complexes, enhancing their convenience and 'attractiveness'. Add to this the food and drink treats that we are encouraged to buy and the ability to share the encounter with groups of friends or indeed groups of strangers and it all combines to provide a unique and compelling experience.

Leaving aside developments in the cost and style of movie-making, the cinema as an entity has progressively and successfully re-invented itself to survive and compete. Threats from the popularity of other forms of entertainment, such as sporting events and concerts, continue of course.

> 'It is for this reason that people choose to attend football matches or indeed watch them at the pub, even when they could watch them at home.'

More significantly, and literally closer to home, are more recent developments in the cost and sophistication of home-entertainment. Whether it is the expanding choice of broadband and digital-enabled TV channels; the responsiveness of today's TV and PC-based interactive games; the reducing cost and availability of DVD or downloaded movies; or the increasing quality of our home audio-visual set-ups with their large flat-screens,

it is hard to see how the cinema can survive in the future. For the price of a family trip to the cinema, for example, you can probably now buy two or three DVD movies or indeed the DVD player to play them on.

But survive I believe the cinema will, in part because of the social dimension or atmosphere that it can offer, enabled through its scale and physical form. It is for this reason that people choose to attend football matches or indeed watch them at the pub, even when they could watch them at home. Indeed, through digital developments, the cinema can now provide an alternative place to better hear and see major sports or music events as they happen (and importantly as part of a crowd) and this may well be key element in its future strategy. Exploiting facilities beyond their original intent and addressing new markets. Providing a unique experience.

Art for art's sake

The evolution of the cinema reminds me that, as I watch my children energetically interact with their Wii applications, I am old enough to remember the original TV-based interactive tennis and space invader games. I am sadly also old enough to remember my collection of vinyl LPs (some of which still sit in boxes in the loft, unloved and unplayed). I was slow to embrace the advent of CDs, mainly because their scale and packaging denied me of one of the main attractions of the LP – its tangibility as a more substantial product, which included the cover and its artwork and associated lyrics and sleeve notes, which was as important to the music collector as the music itself. Exploring the packaging for the first time was just as exciting as hearing the music.

Nowadays, much of this packaging is considered classic and collectable and assumes more value than the freely available music itself. The CD and its scale of packaging never quite matched the value, in this sense, of its predecessor. In a similar way the advent of downloaded music, which has many benefits, may never replace the sense of possessing a tangible music product. Indeed I predict

that such virtual products will need to be more tangible in the future if they are to have a value to the consumer – not least because we increasingly associate digital material as free anyway. I suggest that download-savvy music fans will choose, in the future, to pay a premium to obtain an artist's entire back-collection if it came with its own suitably branded MP3 player (or whatever the latest device will be) along with other memorabilia in its packaging.

In the 'old' days, bands did tours to promote albums, now they give away virtual albums to promote tours. The money is in the shared and physical experience, which is considered a premium over the virtual alternatives.

Back to the workplace

The examples of cinema and popular music from everyday life remind us that the virtual world, enabled by technology, whilst having a distinct and valuable role, especially in terms of accessibility and speed, doesn't always necessarily replace or even effectively compete with the more traditional, physical world. This is especially where physical form or human presence come together to provide an attractive, compelling and emotional experience. Indeed the objective often of virtual alternatives is to be as true to real life as possible. The sophistication of interactive games and developments in *Second Life*[1] existences are testimony to this – presenting both realistic, as well as more fantasy-based, alternative worlds for us to be in. Fantasies aside, why should we settle, in many instances, for second best, when you can have the real thing?

> **'The money is in the shared and physical experience, which is considered a premium over the virtual alternatives.'**

This is good news for the workplace – signalling a definite future which needs to be understood and exploited. Predictions a few decades ago that suggested huge drones of

---

1   *Second Life* – user defined virtual world, where real life, including commerce, is simulated – where avatars (virtual representations of people) interact.

the office workforce would become full-time teleworkers (working entirely from the remoteness of home or a local centre) and have entirely virtual relationships with their colleagues and customers, have never really materialised.

Remember the organisation, mentioned in the previous chapter, which developed comprehensive home-working policies, which its workforce rejected? They valued the experience of coming to the office over being 'home-alone'. Why would they want to do their work in isolation? It would likely be a very monotonous, boring working day without the social interactions they valued so much.

I have also come across many instances where, although certain information is available online through an intranet or indeed the Internet, people choose to meet informally with each other to get that information 'from the horse's mouth'. There is a certain added value in seeing the body language, hearing the antidotes and interacting physically. If such a tailored encounter can take place in comfortable and stimulating surroundings, with nice coffee or food and new and interesting people all around – then even better.

In the 'Expression' chapter I explored the power of design in creating places that are attractive and rewarding. Our interface with physical and visual form has a large bearing on the nature and quality of our experience, but to be really successful, a workplace, or any place for that matter, needs to do more than just look good and create a visual impression.

Success is also about the ability to do what you need to effectively – be that to buy the goods you need, see the people you need to speak to or produce or achieve the outputs and outcomes you desire. The frustration of not meeting these needs will provide a negative experience that will outweigh

> **'There is a certain added value in seeing the body language, hearing the antidotes and interacting physically.'**

any superficial attractiveness. So the future workplace needs to be a pleasingly designed, but highly functional physical place. Part of this functionality will be its ability to attract a critical mass of people to support the social and interaction needs of work and create an atmosphere or culture that is rewarding and compelling.

People and space dynamic

People are very important to atmosphere and experience – remember the football match and concert scenarios – although absence of people (or their noise) can also sometimes provide a desirable atmosphere, think of libraries and even an empty church.

In workplace terms this needs to be reflected in the design, layout and range (or landscape) of worksettings provided, as suggested earlier; but also in how they are used and occupied. Yes, the workplace needs to support quiet, solo, concentrative work but, perhaps more importantly, also the more collaborative, interactive aspects of work in a better way. There are more limited alternatives available here, enabling this to become the workplace's equivalent of its unique selling point (USP). But organisations cannot be complacent about this, as there are still viable physical alternatives for the interactive office workplace.

I remember conducting a space utilisation study[2] for one Birmingham-based organisation, which concluded that workspace utilisation (desks and meeting rooms) was very low but there was a high degree of 'temporarily unoccupied' space – where the occupants were clearly around but not present when observations were made. Further investigation revealed that most of the workforce were choosing to frequent nearby coffee bars and hotels to hold their informal and formal work encounters. It wasn't just the more contemporary surroundings or quality of coffee that enticed them, staff also cited more

2   Refer back to Chapter 2, Figure 2.4.

relevant facilities and levels of service. Clearly the office failed to support their aspirations and needs – and staff voted with their feet.

The soul-less office floors of formalised desking and meeting rooms left behind clearly demonstrated that functionality alone is not enough. The few staff left behind, perhaps tied to their systems and processes, existed in a place that had a 'dead' atmosphere, where long spells of quietness were interrupted by small but unexpected and exaggerated noise, as sound rattled around the empty hard surfaces that prevailed. Places designed for people only work when people are there. Try attending a concert in a large empty arena, it just doesn't work.

The office buzz

Though many of us complain about it, office 'buzz' helps create a productive atmosphere and work experience, where background noise is more controlled and regular. A busy restaurant can sometimes be the perfect place to hold a confidential or intimate conversation. Indeed we often introduce 'white noise' into an office (or music into a restaurant) to fill the 'noise void'.

> **'Clearly the office failed to support their aspirations and needs – and staff voted with their feet.'**

The negative atmosphere created by empty, unused space is an important part of the rationale for introducing an increased sharing of workspace and desks. Aside from the wastefulness and inefficiency, rows of empty desk can provide an unproductive atmosphere and also be potentially frustrating – where the users are restricted to a relatively small piece of space and are unable to make use of the remaining, seemingly available (but assigned) space.

Some of the real project experiences I have shared in this book have emphasised the value and positive aspects of introducing desk-sharing, if properly planned and thought through. Overwhelming the most significant

outcome provides the antidote for the scenario just described – fewer, but better desk or other worksettings facilities – which attract proportionately more people and thus more 'buzz' and a more positive atmosphere than before.

> 'A busy restaurant can sometimes be the perfect place to hold a confidential or intimate conversation.'

I am sure you have, like me, been put off entering an empty restaurant. For one thing, it doesn't suggest that the venue and therefore its food is popular, but it also promises a forgettable night out. The temptation to walk out and go to the much livelier restaurant you have just passed is irresistible. That avoided restaurant could be your failed future workplace if you get it wrong.

The workplace as an experience

Like the cinemas, the workplace cannot, however, leave it to chance that if it creates a functional place to attract people, the rest – in terms of success and survival – will follow. Throughout this book, we have learned of the importance of being responsive and agile, evolving to meet future needs and opportunities, and looking beyond the immediate business of office-work to what is happening in the wider world of commerce, technology developments and lifestyle patterns. The office workplace needs to continually re-assess and re-invent itself – understanding its place in the wider world of work and excel in its important niche role.

It doesn't need to necessarily compete with other virtual and physical work options – indeed better if it can compliment and combine with those options and strengthen its role. For example, providing quality places to support specialist organisational activities or, more significantly, to provide great spaces to support the physical and virtual (for example, with super video-conferencing) interaction of groups of people; or to provide easy and excellent drop-in facilities for nomadic workers who may want to print quality documents, meet colleagues or access specific knowledge.

Most of all, amidst the array and choice of work options for individuals, the workplace is the one place that can provide a sense of belonging in terms of the organisation (or group of organisations, if workspace is shared) and an articulation of related ethos, values and culture. The spiritual and operational 'heart' of an organisation or business community. A place people want to be associated with and be seen in. A place where people want to come and stay and come back to again and again – and bring their friends and business associates with them. Collectively this compelling proposition self-actuates further development and relevance.

Take an objective look around your office environment – what do you see? How functional is it? How effective is it? What does it say? How does it feel to work there? How relevant is it in relation to what's happening all around it? What will your friends or children think of it? And, most importantly, where is it going?

Sit back now – and like I have done in the passage of creating this book, comprehensively re-imagine the office. Forget what you have been used to, that will no longer be good enough. Forget the usual financial, cultural or policy constraints. Forget the baggage we have collected over decades. Start again.

> 'The office workplace needs to continually re-assess and re-invent itself – understanding its place in the wider world of work and excel in its important niche role.'

Think of the real world outside work, as this is the only world we should be operating in. Make work interesting for yourself and others. Make work better. Be happier. Be yourself. Ask your children what they think. Take time to reflect. Take that holiday, if you need to. Do all these things; and do them well.

Now you can rise to the new workplace *challenge!!*

Final Thoughts

'The future is not some place we are going to, but one we are creating. The paths are not to be found, but made…'

John Schurr, futurist

This book has been a bit of a journey for me – perhaps for you too. It has covered a lot of ground. At times, it has perhaps ranted or panicked about where the office workplace needs to go; at other times there seems reassurance that we can be on top of things.

7 Final Thoughts

'*The future is not some place we are going to, but one we are creating. The paths are not to be found, but made...*'

John Schurr, futurist

This book has been a bit of a journey for me – perhaps for you too. It has covered a lot of ground. At times, it has perhaps ranted or panicked about where the office workplace needs to go; at other times there seems reassurance that we can be on top of things.

I am not a workplace expert, in the technical sense, more an observer of office life – with experience as an office user and a consultant adviser, learning many lessons on the way. Above all, I am a normal human being – with a personal and family life outside work to keep me grounded, keep things real. These are the most important qualities I can bring to these workplace considerations. The language and references used, I hope, will enable people of all disciplines and levels within organisations to get engaged and involved in shaping the future workplace.

> **'...the divergence between real life and the office workplace is closing.'**

I have avoided creating a case study book, partly in order to protect the confidentiality of clients, with whom my work can be sensitive and intense at times. I also wanted my project recollections to cover both positive and negative aspects, to make them real and relevant to the arguments. I have tried to acknowledge current developments and trends, but know I can only skim the surface here, especially with technology, where it almost fruitless to try to keep up within the media of a published book.

The main inspiration for this book, however, has come from taking a step well back from everyday work-life and looking at things from a new perspective

and in the context of everyday things, like my children or how we shop or entertain ourselves. I would recommend this to anyone.

I do sense that the divergence between real life and the office workplace is closing. The boundaries are blurring and converging. These worlds can never afford to get out of step again. If the challenge over the past 20 years has been about moving to more open, but appropriately designed, work environments, then the challenge now is to recognise the broader workscape beyond the office, and, importantly, break the psychological tie to the conventional office desk. Only then are we truly liberated to exploit the opportunities.

The new workplace challenge is as much about our mindsets, as any physical or technical transformation. We need to embrace the required changes bravely, but with confidence. I would urge you to focus simply on this attitudinal change (personally and organisationally). It might be uncomfortable for a while; but the rest, I believe, will then follow naturally. I wish us all luck!

Case Study: The Northern Ireland Civil Service

Whilst clearly stating that this is not a case study book, but rather a book of observations and commentary, I find myself wanting to provide at least one case study to 'complete' the book from a readership point of view. To provide an example of how many of the ideas pursued in the book are starting to, reassuringly, manifest themselves in today's office environment.

Although there will be many case studies operating at the extremes of such development, I have chosen the Northern Ireland Civil Service (and its Department of Finance and Personnel office in Clare House, Belfast) as perhaps more typical of where many organisations might be. It also happens to be a current project of mine.

Source: NICS.

Story so far

The Northern Ireland Civil Service (NICS) story is an interesting one, not least because of how far they have travelled in recent years in terms of reform and modernisation. In the workplace sense, little investment had been made to Government stock until recent years, revealing 'time-warp' office scenarios – often uncomfortable, unfit for purpose, highly hierarchical but, nevertheless,

apparently loved by occupants not wanting to move on from the comfort of such familiarity.

Clare House in Belfast is a modern, but redeveloped, three storey open-plan office – with an after-build central atrium created to further open up the office and improve the vertical connectivity within the building. The central areas have become the focus of new break-out spaces, with a *Starbucks* coffee area providing a central hub for informal social and business interaction at ground floor level.

New space and storage standards, modular furniture solutions and shared local facility areas (including printing) support staff of all grades to operate

Source: NICS.

together in this new open working environment. A fairly typical modern office, perhaps, but especially modern and a 'first' for the NICS.

But that is just Phase 1.

Agile workspace

Many of the images provided here focus on Phase 2 which, aligned with the thinking in this book, acknowledges the increasing dynamism of office work

Source: NICS.

and the broader distributed working landscape. Phase 2 is represented by a re-designed ground floor workspace where 'agile workers' operate in a vibrant new shared working environment and adjoining business zone (which is open to visiting staff from any NICS department).

In this space, a range of new worksettings have been established to support individual and collaborative, as well short and long-stay working. Worksettings include desks (most of them larger than before), quiet booths, team tables, diner booths, circular meeting or working pods, stand-up touchdowns and a range of sofa-based spaces. Sharing has enabled a more 'relaxed' and interesting layout and extensive use of graphic features have added to the appeal of this 'showcase' office – emphasising its new role and purpose.

Essentially workers (and yes, there are over a third more now using this space than were previously accommodated) choose their worksetting depending on what they need to

Source: NICS.

Source: NICS.

do and many will change worksettings during the course of the day as they move from one mode of work to another. Laptops, mobile phones/devices and, just as I write, wireless connectivity all feature to support this next phase in office development. As we have learnt from this book, the office is only one part of the life of such agile workers – with most of those involved also supported in working across many locations and at home.

The richness of these workstyle choices set these workers apart from their peers at present and their new office environment is clearly still a destination of choice, despite the broader workplace options, instilling a sense of pride, community and values – sharing here means being a winner, not a loser. New protocols, aptly called 'The rough guide to smooth working' further support the new dynamics. But it didn't all happen by chance, attention to research, consultation and support – the human aspects discussed at length in this book – all feature.

Source: NICS.

Source: NICS.

Change at work

As suggested, this case study is a pilot, a pathfinder, a showcase. The challenge of exploiting these opportunities more widely remains. However, the business case to embrace such changes are, interestingly, more relevant than ever, as organisations in all sectors find an increasing need to 'do more with less', as well as differentiate themselves. The need to win hearts and minds and encourage innovation is also as strong as ever. But this is compelling, energetic change in action, which increasingly is making sense to people because of its connection to the real world! The appetite to go further is abundantly clear. As I constantly tell visitors to Clare House: 'Watch this space, as here we are truly *re-imagining the office*!!!'

Source: NICS.

Banner image, *source*: NICS.

If you have found this book useful you may be interested in other titles from Gower

New Workspace, New Culture
Gavin Turner and Jeremy Myerson
Hardback: 978-0-566-08028-9

How to Market Design Consultancy Services
Shan Preddy
Paperback: 978-0-566-08594-9

Identity
Mark Rowden
Hardback: 978-0-566-08618-2

Design for Sustainability
Tracy Bhamra and Vicky Lofthouse
Hardback: 978-0-566-08704-2

Design for Inclusivity
Roger Coleman, John Clarkson, Hua Dong and Julia Cassim
Hardback: 978-0-566-08707-3

Design for Micro-Utopias
John Wood
Hardback: 978-0-7546-4608-2

Designing for the 21st Century
Tom Inns
Hardback: 978-0-566-08737-0

New Demographics, New Workspace
Jeremy Myerson, Jo-Anne Bichard and Alma Erlich
Hardback: 978-0-566-08854-4

Enterprise 2.0
Niall Cook
Hardback: 978-0-566-08800-1

Visit **www.gowerpublishing.com** and

- search the entire catalogue of Gower books in print
- order titles online at 10% discount
- take advantage of special offers
- sign up for our monthly e-mail update service
- download free sample chapters from all recent titles
- download or order our catalogue